# WELL-BEING
## *for* WOMEN

# WELL-BEING
## *for* WOMEN

## STELLA WELLER

A GODSFIELD BOOK

Library of Congress
Cataloging-in-Publication Data Available

10 9 8 7 6 5 4 3 2 1

Published in 1999 by
Sterling Publishing Company, Inc.
387 Park Avenue South,
New York, N.Y. 10016
© 1999 Godsfield Press
Text © 1999 Stella Weller

Distributed in Canada by Sterling Publishing
c/o Canadian Manda Group,
One Atlantic Avenue, Suite 105,
Toronto, Ontario, Canada M6K 3E7
Distributed in Australia by
Capricorn Link (Australia) Pty Ltd
P O. Box 6651, Baulkham Hills
Business Centre, NSW 2153, Australia

Printed and bound in Hong Kong

Sterling ISBN 0–8069–9919–5

*The publishers wish to thank
the following for the use of pictures:*
Archiv für Kunst und Geschichte pp: 90cb
Bridgeman Art Library pp: 42bl
Hulton Getty pp: 111cb
Image Bank pp: 7, 11cb, 13mt, 22tr, 29tr, 33cb, 47tl,
48ct, 53ct, 59ct, 61ct, 65ct, 66tl, 75tr, 78bl, 83cl,
85tr, 93tl, 103ct, 112r, 115tl, 120/121, 124/125
Rex Features pp: 6cm, 80ct
Science Photo Library pp: 24bl
The Stock Market pp: 10/11, 42cb, 52bl, 87r,
108/109, 117tr, 123br
Tony Stone Images pp: 16tr, 19br, 42tr, 58br, 64cr,
72br, 72ct, 97c, 98bl, 100tr, 101bl, 105br, 106cl,
106tr, 108br, 113cb, 116tr

# CONTENTS

# INTRODUCTION

FOR A VERY LONG TIME, WOMEN HAVE BEEN THE PASSIVE CO-INHABITANTS OF A MALE-DOMINATED WORLD. IN HEALTH THEY HAVE, FOR THE MOST PART, MEEKLY COMPLIED WITH THE DICTATES OF MEN. IN SICKNESS THEY HAVE, WITHOUT QUESTION, FOLLOWED TREATMENTS BASED ON RESEARCH AND STUDIES USING MALE SUBJECTS.

**LEFT** *Women now join together not just socially but also on business and political issues.*

Not surprisingly, women finally began to protest and to assert themselves. They fought for equality in many fields of endeavor and in so doing adopted many "male" lifestyle habits, with unpleasant repercussions. Women began losing the hair on their head, having more heart attacks, and suffering from more stress-related disorders than before.

Fortunately, women have now shifted their focus from wanting to be equal with men to being respectfully conscious of the differences between the two sexes. They acknowledge and enjoy these differences without feeling inferior to men. As a consequence, women are at last beginning to savor true liberation.

**BELOW** *Physical and mental health is important to women of all ages.*

Today, women can view themselves as much more than the sum of their reproductive parts and so take a whole-person approach to their health care. They can relinquish the belief that they have to be everything to everyone. They can, without guilt, confidently

**ABOVE** *Exercise helps achieve overall well-being.*

accept the fact that nurturing themselves is an intelligent prerequisite of effectively caring for others while still being able to do all they have or want to do.

Whether you are an adolescent struggling with your identity and self-esteem; a young adult wrestling with issues such as contraception, sex, sexually transmitted disease, and body image; a working woman with or without children, single or otherwise, trying to be everything to everyone except perhaps yourself; a middle-aged woman fearful of losing your youth or worried about depression, high blood pressure, cancer, or heart disease; or an older woman apprehensive of possible loneliness, *Well-being for Women* is for you.

This book shows you proven strategies for living a joyful, healthy, and productive life. The exercises, techniques, and practical suggestions train and encourage women to draw upon their own natural resources (body, mind, and breath) to help maintain optimum well-being or restore health after illness. Many of the exercises and strategies can be incorporated into even the busiest of schedules to prevent an accumulation of tension and fatigue, to keep energy levels adequate or high, build stamina, self-esteem, and confidence, cope with pain and other stressors, and preserve a state of equilibrium even when under pressure. All the techniques are safe

**ABOVE** *You deserve the right to take control of your own life.*

and enjoyable and do not require manufactured equipment. They provide the tools to help you take charge of your life and to get the best care. You deserve it.

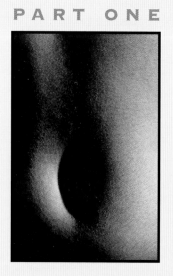

# PART ONE

# ACHIEVING OPTIMUM WELL-BEING

# 1 NURTURING YOURSELF

WOMEN TEND TO PUT THE NEEDS AND WANTS OF OTHERS BEFORE THEIR OWN NEEDS. AS A RESULT, IN TIME, THEY MAY BUILD UP AN INSIDIOUS AND UNCONSCIOUS RESENTMENT TOWARD THE INNOCENT RECIPIENTS OF THEIR CARE. THE DISGRUNTLEMENT THIS CAUSES IS A MAJOR SOURCE OF DIFFICULTY FOR THEM, AND ALSO CAUSES DEPARTURES FROM HEALTH, SUCH AS CHRONIC FATIGUE, DEPRESSION, AND EATING DISORDERS. SACRIFICING THEIR RELATIONSHIP WITH SELF BECAUSE OF THEIR INTERACTIONS WITH OTHERS, THEY QUICKLY DEPLETE THEIR INNER RESOURCES, AND A STATE OF JOYLESSNESS ENSUES.

## LOVING YOURSELF

In order to feel free to nurture yourself as you nurture others, you first need to regard yourself as worthy of nurturing. Psychologists agree that before you can truly love others and are able to give to them freely, you must first love yourself. Loving oneself is not to be equated with selfishness or self-indulgence. Self-love indicates self-respect and self-acceptance. In fact, the more you love yourself, the greater will be your capacity for loving and giving to others.

LEFT *Learn to appreciate the strong ties between your partner, yourself, and your children, as this will do much to boost your sense of well-being.*

BELOW *Being part of a support group, or having one-to-one counseling, can help women who have difficulty in accepting themselves as they are.*

Your body language tells you how you feel about yourself. We are social beings and it is therefore natural to seek, to an extent, the approval of others. However, it is unwise to depend on the acclaim of others to establish or boost your self-esteem. If you continually strive to surround yourself with people who seem to think highly of you, in order to validate your own worth, you risk feelings of loss and emptiness when their apparent admiration is absent.

Involvement in counseling or in a support group can be of great help in building or rebuilding your self-esteem. But there is much that you can do on your own to increase your sense of self-worth.

LEFT *Just being with others enables many women to feel secure and needed. However, it is important not to rely on others to give these feelings of self-worth.*

## SELF-ESTEEM

How you feel about yourself powerfully affects almost every aspect of your life, from the way you function at work to the way you behave in intimate relationships.

When you regard yourself as deserving of care, it is a sign that you have a healthy sense of self-worth, or self-esteem. This quality is perhaps your most important psychological resource. It is therefore worth developing your confidence in your right to a share of the fruits of your efforts.

## BUILDING SELF-ESTEEM

Make two columns on a sheet of paper. In the left-hand column, write a number of sentences, each starting with the words "You are," to reflect statements others have made about you. Opposite each sentence, in the right-hand column, write a corresponding statement starting with "I am," rephrased in a positive manner. For example, opposite "You are slow" you could write "I am careful" or "I am thorough."

Add to the lists from time to time. Review them periodically, as an antidote to dwelling on perceived negative qualities, which would further erode your self-confidence. Be patient and persevere with this.

Make another list. Record on it your interests, needs, and preferences. Also write down your strengths (even if at first you doubt you have any). Think back to a time when someone complimented you on something; or you did something you were proud of, or you know of something you are or were good at.

Add to the list and review it periodically, to develop an awareness of your needs and of who you really are.

A thought repeated often enough can become a reality. Once your self-esteem begins to grow, learn to listen to, and trust, your inner voice. Practice visualization daily while reflecting on something positive, and mentally repeating affirmations such as: "I am a worthwhile human being," or "I love and respect myself," or "Regardless of my shortcomings, I accept myself." See page 52 for ways to combine breathing with visualization, to help you cope with pain and other difficult emotions.

Read biographies of successful people. Most of them have had great struggles and many reasons for failing, if they had not wanted to succeed. Helen Keller, an American girl, became blind and deaf when only 19 months old. But, with the help of her tutor, Anne Sullivan, she graduated from college with honors and wrote several books, to name only two of her outstanding achievements. And in Brazil, Caroline Maria de Jesus, a black mother with only two years of schooling, wrote a diary that has sold more copies than any other Brazilian book in history.

**ABOVE** *Writing a list of your strengths is a step toward self-knowledge and so self-worth.*

**BELOW** *Take inspiration from women who overcome adversity to achieve great things. If they can do it so can you.*

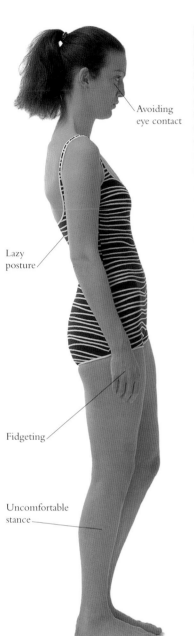

Avoiding
eye contact

Lazy
posture

Fidgeting

Uncomfortable
stance

# SELF-ESTEEM TIPS

◉ Try to look at your failures and mistakes as experiences from which you can learn for your growth and development, not as proof of your incompetence. Tell yourself that you did the best you could at the time, with what you had.

◉ Make a conscious effort to maintain good posture and eye contact, and to speak clearly and directly when talking to others.

◉ Develop a sense of humor and learn to laugh at yourself once in a while.

◉ Learn to accept praise. If, for example, someone pays you a compliment, simply say "Thank you" rather than questioning to yourself why they would want to compliment you at all.

**ABOVE LEFT** *Low self-esteem is reflected in your body language.*

**ABOVE RIGHT** *Use your body language to project a positive, confident persona.*

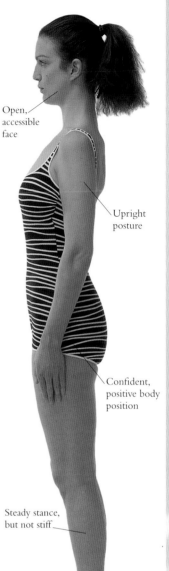

Open,
accessible
face

Upright
posture

Confident,
positive body
position

Steady stance,
but not stiff

**13**

## CARING FOR YOURSELF

One of the soundest decisions you can make is to resolve to stay fit. You can do this largely through adherence to a healthy lifestyle: regular exercise, good nutrition, relaxation, and a support network of friends, relatives, and others who genuinely care about you. It is also important to get enough sleep each night.

Most people in developed countries are sleep-deprived. Reasons include hectic lifestyles, shift work, and mental and physical disorders. Sleep deprivation can have serious consequences, among which are depression, psychosis, and exhaustion. In any event, sleeplessness adversely affects productivity and the quality of life.

If lack of sleep has resulted in ill health, you should always consult your doctor. There are, however, several measures you can take to promote sound, refreshing sleep:

❖ Ensure that the room where you sleep is reasonably quiet, a comfortable temperature, and well ventilated.

❖ You should sleep on a mattress that is firm but not rigid, to give proper support to your spine. Your pillow should support your head adequately. Your bedclothes should not be too heavy as this will impede your circulation. Your sleepwear should be loose and comfortable for ease of movement and breathing.

❖ Avoid drinking alcohol too close to bedtime. Also avoid stimulating reading, television shows, and exercise. Deep, slow, rhythmical breathing or any other technique to induce relaxation is often useful. *(See pages 40–59 for ideas.)*

**ABOVE** *Drinking alcohol before going to bed can disrupt sleep patterns.*

**ABOVE** *Fresh fruit is an essential part of a healthy diet.*

Firm pillow to support the neck and spine

Nightwear in natural fibers

Supportive mattress to prevent back pain

Light bedclothes for comfort and circulation of air

**RIGHT** *Without a good night's sleep it is impossible to face up to life's challenges. Try the tips illustrated here.*

**ABOVE** *Stick to decaffeinated drinks to ensure a good night's sleep.*

❖ Don't go to bed either hungry or with a full stomach. A light carbohydrate snack, however, can help to promote sleep.

Some sleep medications actually detract from the quality of sleep and produce a hangover. If this occurs, you can try herbal remedies, available at herbalists or health food stores. These include: anise, catnip, camomile, deadnettle, hawthorn, hops, hyssop, lady's mantle, lime blossom, passion flower, peppermint, skullcap, St. John's wort, valerian, and wild oats. Each of these can be made into a tea and drunk close to bedtime. Many of the herbs are also available in capsule or tincture form. Before using any herbal remedies, be sure to check with your doctor to ensure that they do not interact with any medications you may be taking.

**RIGHT** *A healthy lifestyle is rewarded by a confidence-boosting physical appearance.*

## ENHANCING YOUR APPEARANCE

Your appearance attests to the care you give to yourself. Part of that care is reflected in three of the most visible parts of your body: your skin, hair, and nails. Because of their visibility, these body parts play an important role in shaping your self-image. Lifestyle habits greatly affect the condition and appearance of all three. Even though they are on the outside of the body and on view, their care is not only an external affair but an internal matter also. To keep them in the best possible health, you need to eat nutritiously, get adequate rest and sleep, exercise regularly, and learn how to cope with stress. *(See pages 20–59 for tips.)* Evidence of their health also partially determines your confidence and your ability to socialize comfortably and, although few skin, hair, and nail disorders are entirely the result of your emotions, there are virtually none that do not profoundly affect your feelings.

Clear, smooth skin

Silky, shiny hair

## CARING FOR SKIN, HAIR, AND NAILS

The condition and appearance of your skin, hair, and nails substantially affect how you feel and function. Their appearance also reflects your nutritional intake. Looking after these structures will enhance your appearance, your self-esteem, and your productivity.

### SKIN CARE

Skin is our protective layer against the outside world, it regulates temperature and fluids, and keeps out germs. It is vital to healthy living to look after your skin very carefully.

❖ In choosing skin-care products for regular use, select those containing nutrients such as vitamins A and E, UVA and UVB filters for protection from the sun, and other non-allergenic ingredients to soothe, condition, and heal the skin.

❖ A diet with adequate fat-soluble vitamins, minerals, and essential fats will help combat the chapping and dryness from cold winter winds.

❖ Avoid perfumed products which could produce an allergic reaction, and choose non-greasy ones that won't clog your pores.

❖ Keep your skin well hydrated by drinking plenty of water.

❖ Apply a moisturizer within three minutes of taking a bath or shower, or washing your face and hands.

❖ Go easy on your use of soap. It takes oil glands about six hours to restore the skin's protective acid

**ABOVE** *If you must sit in the sun, make sure you use sunscreen with a high protection factor.*

mantle balance after a thorough washing with soap and water.

❖ Avoid smoking cigarettes and protect yourself from the sun. Tobacco and over-exposure to the sun are two of the worst offenders in promoting wrinkles.

❖ Avoid alcohol as it reduces the absorption of nutrients and increases the rupture of blood vessels under the skin.

❖ Keep your hands clean and keep them away from your face to help prevent skin eruptions.

❖ Drink mineral water as it flushes the germs out of your body.

**LEFT** *Skin-care products do not have to be expensive to be effective.*

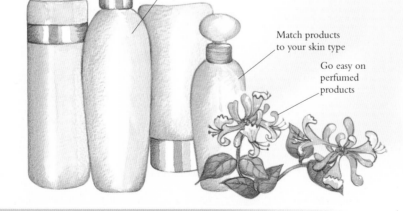

Cleansers are less harsh than soap

Match products to your skin type

Go easy on perfumed products

## HAIR CARE

Experts emphasize the importance of good scalp and hair hygiene for keeping hair on your head and keeping it healthy and attractive. (Losing hair on the head is no longer the monopoly of men due to women taking on the same sort of stressful jobs as men. This additional stress has meant that women are beginning to produce similar levels of androgen hormones to men.) Without good hygiene habits, no treatment for preventing hair loss and maintaining healthy hair can be effective.

❖ Gently massage your scalp every day to enhance the delivery of nutrients through the circulation. Scalp massage also reduces tension build-up in the scalp and keeps it loose – some hair care experts consider keeping the scalp loose as the first essential step in treating hair problems.

❖ Scalp massage promotes relaxation and a feeling of well-being. Massage your scalp with your fingertips for a few minutes whenever you feel tense or under stress.

❖ Do not be afraid of shampooing your hair frequently. Frequent shampooing may, in fact help to slow down some types of hair loss – it does this by keeping your scalp clean and free of accumulated hormonal secretions.

❖ After shampooing your hair, it is important to rinse it thoroughly with cool water. Cool water closes the hair's imbrications (overlapping structures, arranged like tiles or fish scales) and so helps the hair to shine when the light hits it. Closed imbrications also help to protect the inner hair structure.

❖ Do not comb or brush hair when it is wet as it can break easily.

❖ Gently towel-dry wet hair before blow-drying it, and do not over-dry hair as this could cause it to weaken and fall out.

❖ The sun can deplete natural oil coatings on your hair, causing brittleness. If you are sunbathing, try wrapping a towel around your hair to protect it.

❖ Choose a hair style that not only flatters you but which is also easy to care for.

## NAIL CARE

Doctors often look at nails when diagnosing ailments, as they are good indicators of the state of a person's health. For example, white spots on the nails may indicate a zinc deficiency. So, as well as ensuring your intake of nutrients is high, always look after your nails.

**ABOVE** *Well-manicured nails look attractive and so make you feel good.*

❖ No matter how short, keep your nails well shaped.

❖ Do not cut cuticles. After washing, moisturize your hands to prevent the cuticles from cracking.

❖ If you wear nail polish, use oil-based polish removers as other types can dry out your nails.

❖ Wear cotton-lined rubber gloves when washing dishes or clothes, or doing household chores. Wear gardening gloves for outdoor jobs.

❖ Resist the urge to tap impatiently with your fingertips when you feel stressed. This can cause nail damage.

❖ Develop an awareness of what you do with your hands as they are always on view.

**LEFT** *Dull, lifeless hair is a sure sign that there is an underlying health problem.*

## REWARDING YOURSELF

Your willingness to be good to yourself, and to reward yourself for all that you accomplish and everything that you do for others, is an acknowledgment of your self-worth.

The ways in which you can compensate yourself are infinite and beyond the scope of this book. For many women, shopping for clothing and accessories or buying some needed or desired item is what first comes to mind when thinking "What shall I do for me?" However, there may be many other things that appeal to you, such as a long bath or walk alone, where you can have some personal space. Whatever brings a sense of personal satisfaction for each individual is certainly appropriate.

**BELOW** *Taking time to sit and do nothing is an excellent way to recharge your physical and mental batteries.*

**ABOVE** *Escape the busy world with a cup of tea and a good book.*

Optimum health is concerned not only with the physical, but also with the mental, emotional, and spiritual, so, when thinking of ways to reward yourself, do not forget emotional and spiritual fulfilment. Although tangibles are proof that you did or bought something for you, intangibles, though not visible, can sometimes be even more deeply nourishing and satisfying. So consider healthy ways to transport yourself temporarily from the realm of the mundane, to counteract the sometimes humdrum world, and

also ways in which to delight senses that may have become dulled from day-to-day wear and tear.

The following are some suggestions for pampering and otherwise indulging yourself as compensation for jobs well done. Consider them antidotes to the possible tedium, resentment, and disgruntlement of giving to everyone but yourself.

❖ Treat yourself to a day at a beauty salon where you can have a facial, a massage, a hairdo, and a manicure and pedicure. You'll feel like a new woman.

❖ Arrange to have a couple of uninterrupted hours all to yourself. Take a long, luxurious bath while listening to music that relaxes you. Afterward, give yourself a manicure and pedicure. Following this, relax on a sofa and do absolutely nothing; or make some tea and sip it while reading an inspirational or entertaining book.

**LEFT** *Take your partner out on a date. Remind yourselves of what first attracted you to one another and make the evening special.*

❖ Go for a walk in a quiet park or similar place and be aware of your natural surroundings. Stop to look at plants and flowers, or the fish in a pond. Pause to watch the butterflies flitter about. Listen to the birds chirping. Sit for a short period of quiet contemplation by a lake or other beauty spot. If your mind tries to stray to everyday concerns, gently but firmly guide it back to the tranquillity of the present environment.

**BELOW** *Get back to nature. A walk in the country will leave you refreshed and invigorated.*

❖ Have dinner out, alone or with a close companion, followed by a night at the ballet or opera, or go to see a light-hearted musical at a theater.

❖ Go on a one-day tour of a part of the country you would like to learn more about, or go on a river tour. Make sure that it won't be exhausting as it should be an enlightening, uplifting, and refreshing experience for you.

❖ Enrol in a yoga or tai chi course. You should come away from each class feeling rested and relaxed.

**BELOW** *Yoga will give your body a gentle workout while refreshing and calming your spirit.*

❖ Go on a retreat. Some churches, clubs, yoga schools, and other organizations periodically have a weekend retreat conducive to relaxation and recharging of body, mind, and soul.

❖ Pack a picnic basket and invite a friend with interests similar to yours to join you. Choose a pleasing location: a garden, park, or lakeside spot. Keep the conversation light-hearted.

If you have a young family, you will have to make the necessary arrangements to allow you the adequate time for your activity of choice, but whatever the effort it will be worthwhile.

# 2 EATING FOR ENERGY

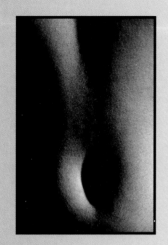

WHAT WE EAT SUPPLIES OUR BODIES WITH FUEL FOR ENERGY. THIS ENERGY IS ESSENTIAL FOR LIFE AND FOR WORK. FOODS ARE MIXTURES OF SUBSTANCES CALLED NUTRIENTS. WHEN FOOD IS METABOLIZED, THE ENERGY FROM EACH OF THE NUTRIENTS IS RELEASED, PROCESSED BY THE DIGESTIVE SYSTEM, AND IT IS THEN TRANSMITTED TO EVERY CELL, TISSUE, AND ORGAN THROUGH THE CIRCULATORY SYSTEM.

## ESSENTIAL NUTRIENTS

A healthy diet should provide all the nutrients you require for good health. All the nutrients work together; no single one can provide everything you need. If you are considering taking nutritional supplements, you should consult a dietitian, nutritionist, or other qualified health professional first.

## WATER

Not usually thought of as a nutrient, water is nevertheless the most important substance we consume. It is the principal constituent of body fluids. It is also the medium by which nutrients are transported to cells and wastes removed are from the body. It is a lubricant and a shock absorber; essential for maintaining the moisture in the discs that cushion the bones (vertebrae) of our spine. It is necessary for proper digestion and for regulating body temperature. It also helps to prevent bladder infections, constipation, and dehydration – a major cause of aging.

All liquids provide water, but best sources include unsweetened juices, non-caffeinated drinks (herbal teas, milk), and mineral water.

LEFT *Drink plenty of water throughout the day to prevent your system becoming sluggish.*

## PROTEIN

Your skin, hair, nails, eyes, and muscles are made of protein. It is the basic structure of all cells and it is essential for the synthesis (building up) of collagen, the "glue" that holds cells together.

There are two types of protein. The first, complete proteins, are obtained chiefly from foods of animal origin, such as meat, poultry, seafood, eggs, and dairy products. They contain a proper balance of the eight essential amino acids (protein-building blocks). The other type, incomplete proteins, lacks some essential amino acids, but, in certain combinations, can be made complete. They are found in grains, pulses (dried beans, peas, and lentils), and seeds. Examples of combinations to render them complete include: rice and pulses; maize (corn) and beans; whole-wheat bread with baked beans.

## AVAILABLE AND UNAVAILABLE CARBOHYDRATES

Available carbohydrates are those that can be metabolized by the body. There are two types of available carbohydrates: simple and complex. In the first category are foods such as refined white rice and sugar. The second category includes whole-grain breads and pasta, fresh fruits, and fresh vegetables. These complex carbohydrate foods help to prevent excess weight and high blood pressure, and help to lower high blood cholesterol levels. A high

complex carbohydrate diet, rather than a high protein one, will provide the best fuel for muscles and the energy needed for peak performance in any endeavor.

Unavailable carbohydrates cannot be broken down by the body and therefore pass through it relatively unchanged. These unavailable carbohydrates make up the bulk of what we call dietary fiber.

Disorders such as colon and breast cancer, colitis, hemorrhoids, constipation, and varicose veins, are much lower among people whose diets are high in fiber than among the general population in developed countries. Fiber is also useful in controlling conditions such as atherosclerosis. It does this by preventing the absorption of cholesterol.

Good sources of dietary fiber include breads and other products that are made from whole grains, fresh fruits, raw vegetables, nuts, and pulses.

**ABOVE** *Try to choose something from each of the main food groups at each meal. A varied diet is more likely to be nutritionally well-balanced.*

## FAT

Fat is seen in a negative light, but, actually, a certain amount of it is needed in the daily diet to provide energy, conserve body heat, and help cells to function normally. Fat supports and protects organs such as the kidneys and the eyes. It is also a medium of transportation for the fat-soluble vitamins (A, D, E, and K).

Good sources of fat include butter, cheese, eggs, milk, and nuts, and also the oils from vegetables, nuts, and seeds such as avocados, olives, peanuts, and sesame and sunflower seeds.

Vitamins and minerals are also essential nutrients, but there are so many of them that they have been given extra room over the next few pages in order to deal with them in detail.

## VITAMINS

Unlike the previous nutrients, vitamins are a group of organic compounds required in small quantities by the body for good health. They cannot be manufactured in the body itself and must therefore be obtained directly from food.

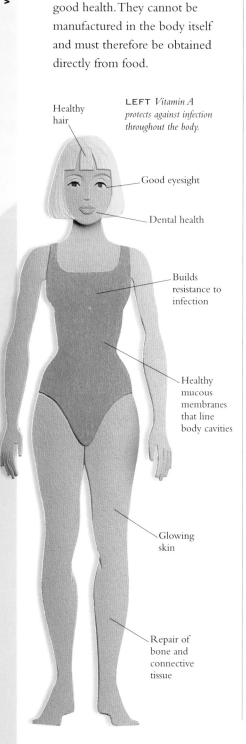

Healthy hair

**LEFT** *Vitamin A protects against infection throughout the body.*

Good eyesight

Dental health

Builds resistance to infection

Healthy mucous membranes that line body cavities

Glowing skin

Repair of bone and connective tissue

**ABOVE** *A balanced diet should provide all the vitamins you need, but if you think you need a supplement take professional advice.*

### VITAMIN A

Vitamin A is an antioxidant that prevents or inhibits the process by which substances combine with oxygen to destroy nutrients. It is an important element in helping to build resistance to infection. It is also necessary for healthy eyesight and for the proper repair of bones and connective tissue. It is essential for the health of the skin, hair, teeth, gums, and mucous membranes that line body cavities and tubular organs.

Vitamin A occurs in two forms: preformed vitamin A (called retinol), which is found in foods of animal origin; and provitamin A (known as carotene) which is provided by foods of both animal and plant origin.

Good sources of vitamins include fresh vegetables, particularly intensely green and yellow ones such as broccoli and carrots, and fresh fruits, especially apricots, cantaloupe melons, papaya, and peaches; also milk, milk products, and fish liver oils.

**ABOVE** *Vitamin A is needed for growth and repair, so include oily fish and green or yellow fruit and vegetables in your diet.*

## THE B VITAMINS

This complex of more than 20 vitamins is essential for maintaining a healthy nervous system and for counteracting the effects of stress. These vitamins help to prevent and fight infections and preserve the health of the skin, hair, and nails.

ABOVE *Grains and cereals are good sources of the B vitamins, which are essential for a healthy metabolism.*

The B vitamins may be obtained from brewer's yeast, fresh fruits and vegetables (notably green leafy ones), pulses, liver, eggs, milk, nuts, seeds, wheat germ, whole grains, and cereals. They are also synthesized (changed into a useable form) by intestinal bacteria.

All the B vitamins work together and are best obtained as a complex. The following are very important:

Vitamin B1 (thiamine) is essential for mental health. It keeps the nervous system, the heart, and other muscles of the body functioning normally and helps prevent fatigue. It also aids appetite and is needed for proper digestion.

RIGHT *B vitamins are present in animal and vegetable products, so a balance of both will increase your chances of obtaining the nutrients you need.*

Vitamin B2 (riboflavin) works with other substances to metabolize proteins, carbohydrates, and fats. It aids vision and relieves eye fatigue, and is also necessary for healthy skin, hair, and nails.

Vitamin B3 (niacin) is an antioxidant. It helps to maintain a healthy digestive system and is important for good circulation and healthy skin.

Vitamin B6 (pyridoxine) is necessary for maintaining good resistance to disease, the proper assimilation of protein and fat, and the production of hormones. It also helps to combat depression and has been found useful in treating premenstrual syndrome (PMS). In addition, it acts as a natural diuretic (an agent that increases the secretion of urine). An interesting and not very well known fact about vitamin B6 is that, along with two other B vitamins (B9 and B12), it helps to prevent a high homocysteine level, which is now considered a risk factor in heart disease. (Homocysteine refers to a group of proteins that are believed to damage the inner walls of arteries when their levels become too high.)

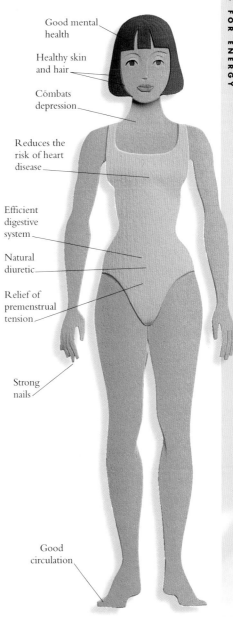

Good mental health

Healthy skin and hair

Combats depression

Reduces the risk of heart disease

Efficient digestive system

Natural diuretic

Relief of premenstrual tension

Strong nails

Good circulation

ABOVE *If you choose to take a supplement of B vitamins, select one that is a complex, for top to toe benefits.*

Vitamin B9 (folate; folic acid) helps to prevent anemia and keeps the immune system functioning effectively. It is also essential in pregnancy to prevent certain birth defects. Vitamin B9 is believed to be important in helping to prevent the build-up of homocysteine (see vitamin B6).

Vitamin B12 (cyanocobalamin) is essential for the production and regeneration of red blood cells. It also helps to maintain the health of the nervous system and to improve concentration and memory. It is also important for the proper utilization of proteins and carbohydrates.

Vitamin B12 is synthesized (changed into a form that the body can absorb) by intestinal bacteria. Like vitamins B6 and B9, it is believed to play a protective role in heart health (see vitamin B6). In view of the crucial part this vitamin plays in the formation of red blood cells, and of women's increased need for blood during their reproductive cycle, supplements of vitamin B12 for vegans are vitally important. Vegans should pay particular attention to this, and talk to their doctor if at all concerned.

**ABOVE** *The body cannot store vitamin C, so have a daily intake of fresh fruits and vegetables.*

## VITAMIN C

Vitamin C is an antioxidant, which helps to retard the potentially destructive effects of oxygen. It is essential for the formation of collagen, which holds cells together. It is important for healthy blood circulation and it is also an antistress vitamin. Vitamin C helps to prevent or relieve the symptoms of a common cold and reduces the effects of some allergy-producing substances. It is useful in alleviating uncomfortable hot flushes during the menopause. It is generally thought that vitamin C also gives some protection against breast cancer.

Included among the best vitamin C sources are fresh fruits such as berries and citrus fruits, rosehips (the seed pods of wild roses), and fresh vegetables – for example, cabbage, peppers, and mustard and cress.

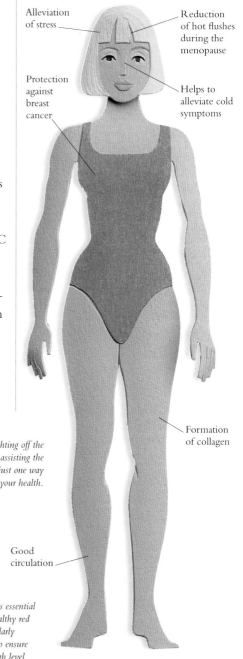

Alleviation of stress

Reduction of hot flushes during the menopause

Protection against breast cancer

Helps to alleviate cold symptoms

Formation of collagen

Good circulation

*RIGHT Fighting off the common cold by assisting the immune system is just one way vitamin C protects your health.*

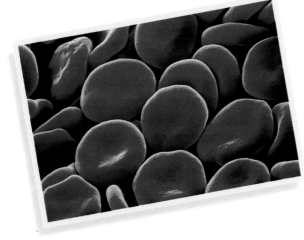

**LEFT** *Vitamin B12 is essential for the formation of healthy red blood cells. It is particularly important for women to ensure they have a high enough level of this vitamin.*

Prevention of
eye inflammation

Healthy
teeth

Absorption
of other
nutrients

Growth
and repair
of bones

RIGHT *Vitamin D,*
*"the sunshine vitamin,"*
*is essential for the*
*absorption of calcium*
*and phosphate.*
*However, in supplement*
*form it can be harmful*
*so consult a professional*
*before taking it.*

## VITAMIN D (CALCIFEROL)

Vitamin D regulates the absorption
of calcium from the intestines and
facilitates the assimilation of
vitamin A. Along with vitamins A
and C, it can help to ward off colds,
and it is also useful in relieving
inflammation of the eyes.

Vitamin D may be obtained
through the action of sunlight
on the skin and from vitamin
D-enriched milk,
butter, eggs, fish,
and fish liver oils.

RIGHT *Vitamin*
*D is found in*
*whole milk, oily*
*fish, butter, and*
*fortified margarine.*

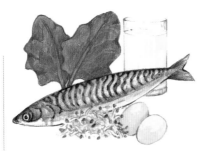

ABOVE *Oily fish, leafy green*
*vegetables, and egg yolk are particularly*
*good sources of vitamin K.*

## VITAMIN E (TOCOPHEROL)

An antioxidant like vitamins A and
C, this vitamin is also considered an
antistress nutrient. It is an effective
vasodilator (it increases the diameter
of blood vessels and so facilitates
blood flow). In addition, it helps to
prevent the formation of blood clots
and it is a natural diuretic. Vitamin
E can slow down cellular aging and
so help you to stay looking young.
It combats fatigue, protects against
pollution, and is also useful in
easing menopausal hot flushes.

Good vitamin E sources include
almonds and other nuts, broccoli,
Brussels sprouts, eggs, fresh fruits,
green leafy vegetables, pulses,
seeds, unrefined oils, wheat
germ, and whole grains.

RIGHT *The left-hand*
*side of this diagram show*
*some of the important*
*benefits of vitamin E.*

Prevention of
blood clots

Natural
diuretic

Slowing of
cellular aging

## VITAMIN K

Vitamin K promotes proper blood
clotting and so helps to prevent
excessive bleeding. It is also
required for the production of the
protein matrix upon which calcium
is deposited to form bone. (A matrix
is the basic substance from which
something develops or is made.)

A varied, wholesome diet usually
furnishes an adequate quantity of
vitamin K for normal requirements.
Particularly good food sources
include alfalfa sprouts, cow's milk,
egg yolk, fish liver oils, green leafy
vegetables, and kelp (a type of
seaweed). Further vitamin K
sources are soy and sunflower oils
and other unrefined vegetable oils.

ABOVE *Broccoli,*
*nuts, and seeds add*
*vitamin E to the diet.*

Essential for
the formation
of bones

Promotion of
proper blood
clotting

LEFT *The right-hand*
*side of this diagram shows*
*some of the important*
*benefits of vitamin K.*

LEFT *Calcium-rich foods will help to strengthen teeth and bones, to combat stress and enhance the nervous system.*

## MINERALS

Minerals are chemical elements, other than carbon, hydrogen, oxygen, and nitrogen, which are required by the body.

### BORON

Boron is a trace mineral that has been shown to safeguard calcium in the body. It is believed that boron is necessary for activating vitamin D and some hormones (such as estrogen). It may also be useful in reducing the discomfort of menopausal hot flushes and controlling atherosclerosis (the narrowing of the arteries, which affects postmenopausal women).

Consuming boron-rich foods is the safest way to ensure an adequate intake of this mineral. Foods that are rich in boron include fresh fruits and vegetables such as apples, grapes, alfalfa, cabbage, peas, and snap beans; also almonds, dates, hazelnuts, peanuts, prunes, raisins, and soy beans.

### CALCIUM

Calcium is an antistress mineral, needed for the proper functioning of nervous tissue. It is required for good muscle tone, sound bones (lack of calcium has been linked to the development of osteoporosis), and teeth, and for a healthy cardiovascular system (heart and blood vessels). Calcium also helps to metabolize iron and is useful in combating insomnia.

The best food sources of calcium include blackstrap molasses, carob powder, citrus fruits, dried beans and figs, green vegetables, milk and milk products, peanuts, sesame seeds, soybeans, sunflower seeds, and walnuts. It is worth also noting that foods such as beets, rhubarb, and spinach, which all contain significant amounts of oxalate, can actually cause a decrease in the absorption of calcium.

### COBALT

Cobalt is part of vitamin B12 and is therefore essential for healthy red cells.

Good cobalt sources include green leafy vegetables, kelp, torula yeast, and whole grains grown in mineral-rich soils.

### COPPER

Copper helps in the proper functioning of nervous and connective tissue. It is also essential for healthy blood and for the utilization of vitamin C.

Good food sources of copper include green leafy vegetables, whole-grain products, pulses, nuts, and prunes.

ABOVE *Cobalt is a constituent of vitamin B12, essential for healthy nervous system, red blood cell formation, and physical growth.*

LEFT *Eating boron-rich foods will safeguard calcium in the body.*

LEFT *Copper plays an important part in the development of the nervous system and in food metabolism.*

## IODINE

Iodine is needed to keep the thyroid gland healthy (this gland controls the body's metabolism). Iodine is also needed for energy and may also be useful in weight control. It promotes mental alertness and helps to keep skin, hair, and nails healthy. Natural iodine sources include broccoli, cabbage, carrots, garlic, lettuce, onions, pineapple, and foods grown in iodine-rich coastal soil, such as the Gulf of Mexico.

ABOVE *Too little iodine can cause thyroid problems, affecting the metabolism.*

## IRON

Iron is necessary for the proper utilization of the B vitamins and for the assimilation of vitamin C. It is also required for healthy blood and a sound immune system.

Good sources of iron include blackstrap molasses, brewer's yeast, Brussels sprouts, cauliflower, dried fruits, egg yolk, kiwi fruit, leafy vegetables, seaweed, seeds, Sharon fruit (persimmon), strawberries, watermelon, wheat germ, and whole grains. It is best to avoid taking an iron supplement (or a multivitamin supplement containing iron) unless it has been prescribed by a doctor as excess iron can accumulate in the body and interfere with immunity.

ABOVE *Magnesium is important in the development of bones and in the function of nerves and muscles.*

## MAGNESIUM

Magnesium is an antistress mineral, which is useful in combating depression and insomnia. It is essential for the synthesis of protein and for the utilization of several other nutrients. Magnesium is also needed for sound bones and for a healthy nervous system and cardiovascular system.

Good magnesium sources include fresh fruits and vegetables grown in mineral-rich soils, almonds and other nuts eaten fresh from the shell, seeds, and whole-grain cereals.

## POTASSIUM

Potassium works with sodium (another mineral) to regulate the body's water balance and to keep the heart rhythm normal. It is also needed for nerves and muscles to function properly. Potassium can promote clarity of thinking by improving oxygen supply to the brain.

The best sources include bananas, citrus fruits, eggplants, mint leaves, nuts, pears, peas, peppers, watercress, watermelon, and whole-grain cereals.

BELOW *Potassium helps control the body's fluid balance.*

BELOW *Iron is essential to hemoglobin, the oxygen-carrying component of red blood cells.*

## SELENIUM

Selenium is an antioxidant. It is required for healthy blood circulation and to preserve the youthful elasticity of the body's tissues. Selenium may also be useful in relieving certain menopausal discomforts such as hot flushes. Selenium, moreover, is thought to give some protection against breast cancer.

The best food sources include apple cider vinegar, asparagus, brewer's yeast, eggs, garlic, mushrooms, sesame seeds, unrefined cereals, wheat germ, whole grains, as well as whole-grain products.

**ABOVE** *Selenium protects cell membranes from damage that can lead to disease.*

**BELOW** *Vanadium might be useful to those with high cholesterol levels.*

**ABOVE** *Silicon is considered one way to give a top to toe boost to your whole body.*

## SILICON (SILICA)

Silicon is considered an anti-aging nutrient that gives life to skin, luster to hair, and beautiful finishing touches to the whole body. It is also needed for healthy bones and connective tissue and for the normal functioning of the adrenal glands. (These glands, which are located above the kidneys, are involved in various stress reactions.) In addition, silicon is required for the overall health of the heart and blood vessels.

Foods made from natural buckwheat are a rich source of silicon, but the mineral may also be obtained from fresh fruits and vegetables and from whole grains and cereals.

## VANADIUM

A lack of vanadium is thought to cause the storage of excess calories in the form of fat, and even a marginal deficiency may result in weight gain. Vanadium is also involved in the utilization of sugar and may be useful in preventing the build-up of cholesterol.

This mineral is found chiefly in fish, but it is also present in radishes, olives, and vegetable oils such as soy, corn, and olive. Vanadium can easily be toxic if taken in synthetic form.

## ZINC

Zinc is essential for the proper functioning of more than 70 enzymes (protein that regulates reaction rates) in the body. Zinc is important for a healthy immune system and for mental and physical health in general. It helps muscles to contract normally, it aids the formation of insulin, promotes mental alertness, and keeps skin, nails, and blood circulation healthy.

Foods rich in zinc include brewer's yeast, cheese, eggs, green and fava beans, mushrooms, non-fat dried milk, nuts, pumpkin seeds, soybeans, sunflower seeds, wheat germ, and whole-grain products.

**RIGHT** *Zinc helps process protein, carbohydrates, and fat, it promotes growth, and is important to the immune system.*

## NUTRIENT ANTAGONISTS

It is important to bear in mind that just as we can help our bodies by taking in vitamins, minerals, etc, we can also hinder the absorption of those nutrients. An antagonist is something that counteracts the action of something else. Nutrient antagonists act against the health-promoting properties of the vitamins, minerals, and other nutrients obtained from the food you eat. Notable nutrient antagonists include:

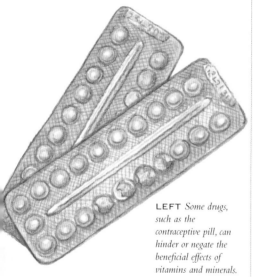

LEFT *Some drugs, such as the contraceptive pill, can hinder or negate the beneficial effects of vitamins and minerals.*

❖ The regular intaking of acetysalicylic acid (aspirin) increases the need for vitamin C.
❖ Contraceptive pills can act against the B-complex vitamins and zinc.
❖ Rancid oils and other rancid food can destroy the vitamin E in the body.
❖ Some commercial laxatives, if they are used regularly, cause deficiencies of vitamin C and the B vitamins.

❖ Smoking destroys vitamin C and the B vitamins and reduces vital oxygen supplies to the tissues.
❖ High alcohol intake is antagonistic to several of the essential vitamins and minerals that the body needs. It also increases the body's overall appetite by lowering blood sugar level. Alcohol also causes weight gain; it supplies extra calories without providing the body with any useful nutrients at all.

RIGHT *Take care of what you put into your body, so that you can be aware of any conflicts that might arise and can take action accordingly.*

ABOVE *Taking regular exercise not only makes you feel good, it also boosts your metabolism and helps nutrients to do their job properly.*

❖ Too much caffeine promotes dehydration and robs the body of certain essential nutrients such as calcium.
❖ Lack of exercise impairs the delivery of vital nutrients to the body's tissues.

## SPECIAL NEEDS

A woman's nutritional needs will vary at each stage of her life. A pregnant woman, for example, has a greater need for certain nutrients than a non-pregnant or postmenopausal woman.

ABOVE *Teenage girls need to watch their diet. As self-image becomes increasingly important, the pressures to be slim might mean they miss out on essential nutrients.*

### ADOLESCENCE

During this phase of rapid growth and numerous physiological changes, the need for almost all nutrients increases. Particularly important at this stage are the B vitamins, vitamin C, and the minerals iron, calcium, and zinc.

### PREGNANCY

Calcium is extremely important as the baby utilizes available calcium for its own needs. And if your calcium stores are inadequate, you could develop osteoporosis. You may also be at risk of pre-eclampsia, a toxemia of pregnancy characterized by unpleasant symptoms including high blood pressure. Insufficient calcium can also lead to leg cramps. Try to eat at least one carton of low-fat yogurt a day. Not only will it provide calcium, it will also help to protect you from vaginal infections, which are common in pregnancy.

Folic acid (vitamin B9) is crucial for the prevention of birth defects, particularly in the first month following conception. Women who have regularly used birth control pills may have lower folic acid stores than those not using oral contraceptives and they should consult their doctor about possible supplementation, preferably before becoming pregnant.

Avoid drinking alcohol in pregnancy as it may lead to fetal alcohol syndrome, a severe form of retardation. Restrict consumption of caffeinated drinks, such as coffee, to avoid possible birth defects. Caffeine interferes with the body's absorption of the nutrients your baby needs. A caffeine addiction can also be passed on to your baby.

BELOW *Don't let bizarre food cravings deter you from having a healthy and well-balanced diet during your pregnancy.*

ABOVE *Some symptoms of the menopause can be alleviated by modifying your diet to boost your intake of vitamin E and calcium.*

### MENOPAUSE

Women in Japan and other Asian countries rarely complain of symptoms like hot flushes. This has been attributed to their liberal use of soybeans and their by-products (such as tofu and miso), which are abundant in plant estrogens (phytoestrogens).

Asian women also frequently use the herb dong quai to help relieve unpleasant menopausal symptoms, and they sip ginseng tea, another source of phytoestrogens. Women in the Western world often rely on vitamin supplements to help control hot flushes. If you wish to take them, supplements of vitamin E and the B-complex vitamins are particularly useful. Keeping your fat intake low and your calcium intake high can also help.

## NUTRITION CHECKLIST

It is extremely important to look after your nutritional needs, no matter what stage of life you are at, and the following checklist gives you some basic guidelines.

❖ Eat a substantial breakfast to give you energy for the day.

**ABOVE** *Fruit juice, cereals with lowfat milk, followed by whole wheat toast makes a nutritious start to the day.*

❖ Make sure you eat plenty of complex carbohydrate foods.

❖ Reduce your overall fat intake by trying the following things: trim visible fat from meat; remove skin from poultry; steam, broil, or poach foods; use butter and margarine sparingly; buy lowfat milk, cottage cheese, and hard cheeses with reduced fat levels. Also, try eating fresh fruit for your dessert rather than pastries.

❖ Don't be seduced by high-protein diets. They always impose heavy demands on the body and may in fact compromise the immune system. They also cause an increased excretion of nutrients such as calcium and will create a greater need for others in your body, such as the B vitamins.

❖ Increase your intake of non-meat proteins such as grains and pulses.

❖ Make sure you restrict your use of salt (sodium), before, during, and also after cooking. A high-sodium intake has been linked to high blood pressure (hypertension). Sodium may also promote the excretion of calcium.

❖ Don't eat too many convenience foods, which lack essential nutrients. Read the labels: avoid foods with added salt, sugar, and fat.

❖ Avoid alcohol and caffeine. Drink water, herbal teas, lowfat milk, unsweetened fruit juices, or vegetable juices instead.

**ABOVE** *If you need a snack, go for fruit juice or crunchy vegetables rather than cookies and candy bars.*

❖ If you experience low blood sugar (hypoglycemia), eat five or six small meals evenly spaced throughout the day, rather than three larger meals, to help maintain adequate blood sugar levels.

❖ Slow down! Eat slowly and savor your food.

**RIGHT** *Make time to sit and enjoy a meal that offers a balance of protein, carbohydrate filler, and a variety of fresh vegetables, rather than grazing on convenience foods or "ready-meals."*

# 3 BODYWORK

WOMEN WHO TAKE REGULAR EXERCISE CAN EXPECT TO ENJOY HEALTH- IER, HAPPIER, AND MORE PRODUCTIVE LIVES THAN WOMEN WHO PARTICIPATE IN LITTLE OR NO ACTIVITY. REGULAR EXERCISE HELPS TO MAINTAIN HEALTHY BLOOD AND LYMPH CIRCULATION. IT IS THROUGH THE BLOOD THAT ESSENTIAL NUTRIENTS ARE DELIVERED TO ALL THE BODY'S CELLS AND ANTIBODIES ARE CARRIED TO ANY SITES OF DISEASE IN ORDER TO PROMOTE HEALING. TAKING PART IN SOME FORM OF PHYSICAL ACTIVITY ON A REGULAR BASIS HELPS US TO OVERCOME STRESS AND TENSION AND IT WILL ALSO ENCOURAGE A SENSE OF WELL-BEING.

## BENEFITS OF EXERCISE

Exercise helps to preserve good muscle tone, control weight, and reduce the rate of cell breakdown, which is related to aging and the onset of autoimmune diseases such as lupus (*see page 118*).

As a stress reliever, exercise is unsurpassed by any other single activity, except perhaps the regular practice of relaxation techniques. Reducing stress is known to influence the state of mind and is of value in coping with disorders such as insomnia, anxiety, depression, and pain. In short, regular exercise, by contributing substantially to overall fitness, increases a woman's energy and productivity since fewer days are lost to illness.

Although the many advantages of exercising regularly are well known, people frequently plead lack of time as an excuse for neglecting this important component of good health and well-being. It is with this in mind that the mini-workout on page 36 has been devised. Along with a few simple warm- ups to start with and a short cool- down period afterward, the exercises take a mere 15 minutes, if that is all the time you can spare.

ABOVE *Just 15 minutes' exercise a day will reap health benefits, so lack of time is no excuse!*

The exercises in the mini-workout provide further benefits, in keeping with the whole-person, mind-body approach to health care. Because they are done with full attention given to each movement, in synchronization with regular breathing, they help to develop concentration. They also help you to relax by temporarily diverting attention from any troubling environmental stimuli. In this way they encourage a "fine tuning-in" to yourself, to alert you to any departure from good health.

BELOW *Joining an exercise class with a friend can provide an extra incentive to keep going – and will ensure that you enjoy the experience as well!*

## PREPARING TO EXERCISE

Choose a quiet, well-ventilated place for your exercise. It is best to make sure that the surface you practice on is even and padded (a non-skid mat, a carpeted floor, or a lawn is suitable). This surface is referred to as the "mat" in all the following exercise instructions.

Try to practice about the same time every day or every other day. Exercising in the morning gives you the energy and alertness that will enhance productivity during the day ahead. Exercising in the evening can be a good way of dissolving the day's accumulated tension and will also help to promote sound, refreshing sleep.

Try to set aside at least a half-hour a day for exercise. You can divide this into two 15-minute sessions if you prefer.

Practice on an empty or near-empty stomach. Wait for about an hour after a light snack before you do any exercise.

When resuming exercising after an illness or other interruption, do so very gradually and patiently.

### HELPFUL HINT

⊙ It is a good idea to check with your doctor before embarking on any type of exercise program at all.

## WARM-UPS

Most of these warm-ups can be integrated into daily schedules, no matter how busy you are.

### THE NECK

**1** Sit or stand comfortably, maintaining good posture. Relax your jaw, shoulders, and arms. Close your eyes or, if you prefer, you can keep them open. Breathe regularly through your nostrils.
**2** Imagine a large figure eight lying on its side in front of you.
**3** With your nose, trace its outline in a clockwise direction, three to five times. Rest.
**4** Repeat this exercise, this time with a counter-clockwise motion, three to five times. Rest.

### THE SHOULDERS

**1** Sit or stand comfortably, maintaining good posture. Relax your jaw and arms. Close your eyes or keep them open if that is what you would prefer. Breathe regularly through your nostrils.
**2** Make slow, smooth circles with your shoulders, in a forward-to-backward direction, three to five times. Rest.
**3** Make slow, smooth circles with your shoulders, in a backward-to-forward direction, three to five times. Rest.

**RIGHT** *Loosen your shoulders and feel the tension slip away. This is a great exercise to do on a regular basis to ease stress.*

---

## WARMING-UP

Warm-ups are very important before any form of exercise. They help to:
⊙ Reduce stiffness.
⊙ Increase body temperature.
⊙ Improve circulation.
⊙ Prevent pulls and strains to muscles and joints.
⊙ Prevent the build-up of tension that can often lead to various discomforts and to pain in many different parts of the body.

**ABOVE** *Trace a figure eight in the air with your nose to warm up your neck muscles*

**LEFT** *Do this warm-up exercise in both directions before you start your main exercise routine.*

## THE UPPER BACK

This is an excellent exercise to do after you have been sitting at a desk, computer, or machine, or if you have been doing any activity that requires bending forward for some time.

**1** Stand tall, maintaining good posture; or sit on a stool or other prop, where you can swing your arms freely behind you. Relax your jaw. Close your eyes or keep them open. Breathe regularly through your nostrils.

**2** Inhale and swing your arms behind you – then interlace the fingers of one hand with those of the other.

**3** Maintain your upright position and raise the still-clasped hands as high as you comfortably can (you may even bend backward slightly). Keep breathing regularly.

**4** Resume your starting position and rest.

**5** Repeat the exercise once or twice.

**ABOVE** *With practice you will soon be able to push your knees to the ground for a deeper stretch.*

## THE LEGS

**1** Sit with your back straight and your legs stretched out in front of you. Relax your shoulders. Breathe regularly through your nostrils.

**2** Put the soles of your feet together and fold your legs, bringing them as comfortably close to you as you can. Clasp your hands around your feet.

**3** Alternately lower and raise your knees as many times as you wish, like a butterfly flapping its wings.

## THE WHOLE BODY

**1** Sit comfortably on your mat and breathe regularly through your nostrils.

**2** Bend your legs and rest the soles of your feet flat on the mat, near your bottom.

**3** Pass your arms under your knees and hug your thighs.

**4.** Tilt your head downward, tuck in your chin, and make your back as round as you possibly can.

**5** Inhale and kick upward so that you roll onto your back.

**ABOVE** *This rock-and-roll motion will warm up your entire body.*

**6** Exhale and roll yourself back into a sitting position. Do not land heavily on your feet as it will jar your spine.

**7** Repeat the alternate rocking backward and forward, as many times as you wish, in smooth succession. Rest.

**LEFT** *Opening out the chest muscles will relieve tension in the upper back.*

## MINI-WORKOUT

This workout consists of 10 body movements, each flowing into the next in graceful sequence. They provide forward and backward bends and stretches for the arms and legs, to maintain flexibility of the spine and to tone up the muscles of the limbs and torso. They are complemented by the spinal twist and lateral stretch on pages 38–39.

**1** Stand tall, with your body weight equally distributed between your feet. Relax your arms at your sides. Breathe regularly through your nostrils. This is your starting position for the mini-workout.

**2** Inhale and raise your arms overhead. Carefully bend backward slightly; tighten your buttocks to protect your back.

**3** Exhale and then slowly bend forward; place your hands beside your feet. Keep your knees straight if you can.

**4** Inhale and look up. Keep your hands by your feet and step backward with your left foot; point your toes forward.

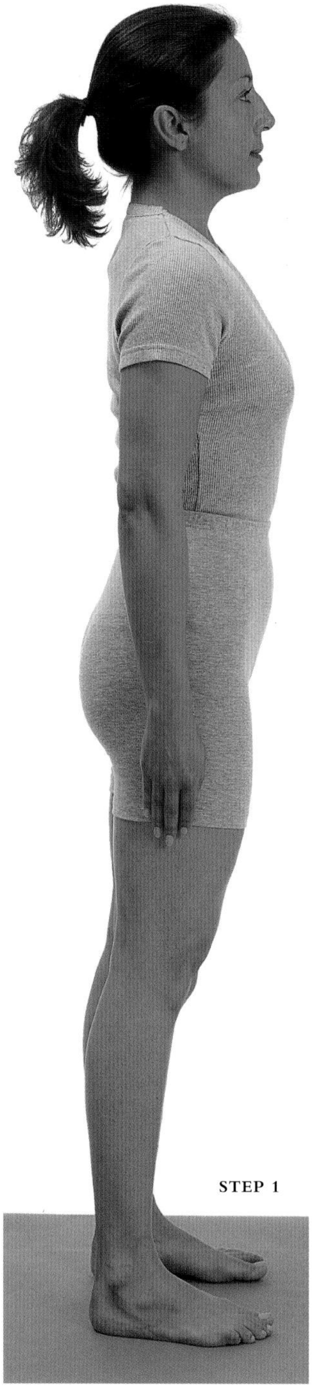

STEP 1

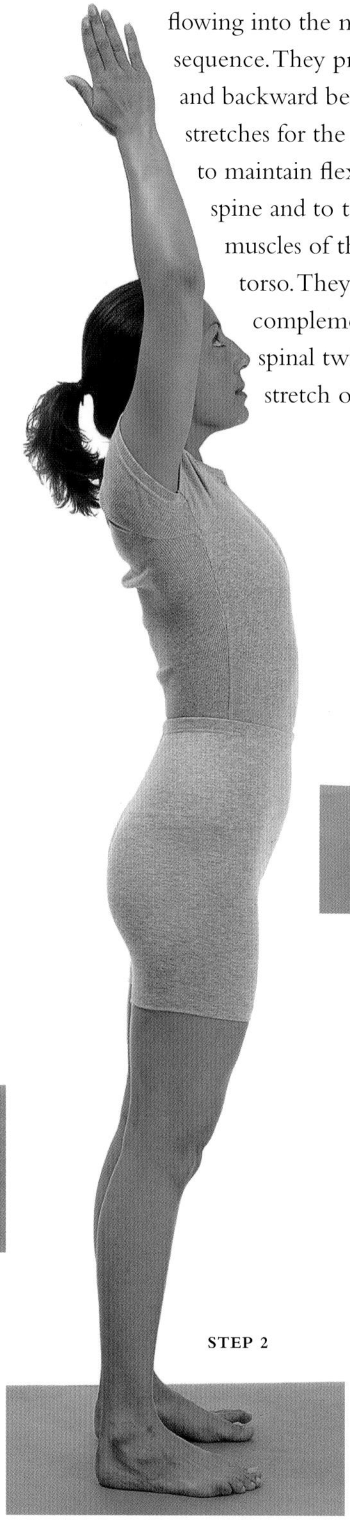

STEP 2

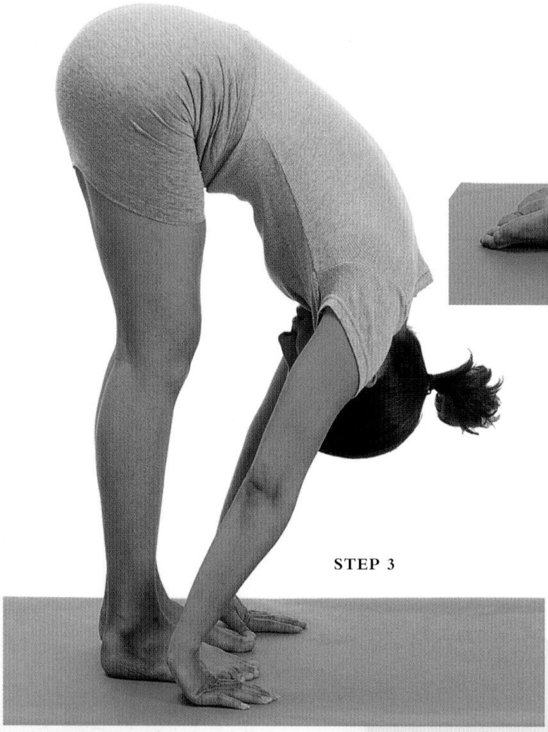

STEP 3

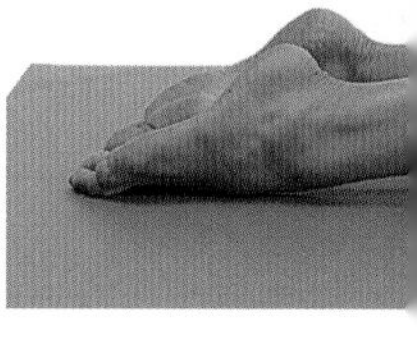

**5** Hold your breath and step backward with your right foot. Lower your body, keeping it level from head to heels.

**6** Exhale and lower your knees to the mat; also lower your chin or forehead, whichever is more comfortable. Relax your feet; push your toes backward. Make sure you breathe regularly.

**7** Inhale and lower the rest of your body to the mat. Carefully arch your back. Keep your head back and your hands pressed to the mat. Relax your feet.

**8** Exhale. Put your weight onto the balls of your feet. Push against the mat with your hands to help to raise your hips. Keep your arms as straight as you can. Hang your head down. Aim your heels toward the mat but do not force them down.

**9** Inhale and look up. Rock forward onto your toes and step between your hands with your left foot.

**10** Exhale. Step between your hands with your other foot and come into a forward-bending position, as in step 3.

**11** Inhale, come up carefully into a standing position and move smoothly into a backward-bend, with arms raised, as in step 2.

**12** Resume your starting position as in step 1. Lie down and rest, or repeat the entire series of exercises (steps 1–12) one or more times. Rest afterward. (steps 5, 9, 10, 11, 12, not illustrated).

**STEP 6**

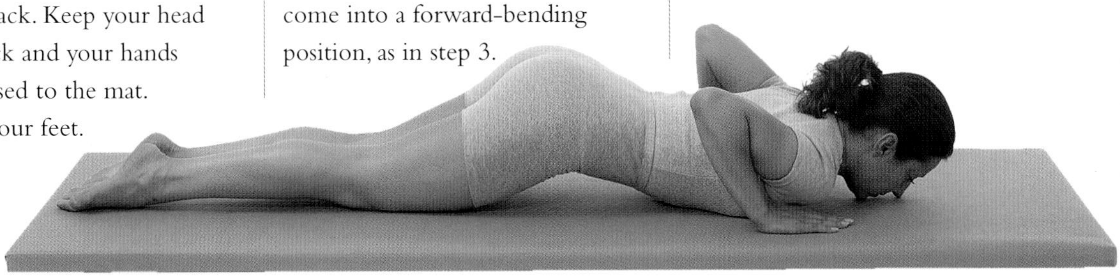

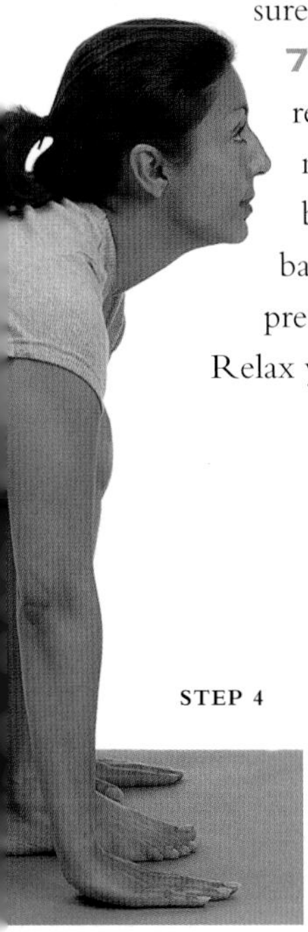

**STEP 4**

**STEP 7**

**STEP 8**

## SPINAL TWIST

This exercise requires maximum torsion (twisting) of your entire spine, first to one side and then to the next. It is excellent for keeping your spine flexible and prevents unnecessary aging. It is also beneficial to spinal nerves and circulation.

The spinal twist also exercises the back muscles and beneficially stimulates the kidneys and the adrenal glands, thus "recharging the batteries" of the body's cells. In addition, this exercise conditions three of the four sets of muscles that form the "abdominal corset."

**1** Sit up straight, with your legs stretched out in front of you.
**2** Bend your left knee. Rest your foot on the mat near the outside of your right knee.
**3** Exhale and slowly and smoothly twist your upper body to the left. Rest your palms on the mat at your left side. Turn your head and look over your left shoulder.
**4** Maintain this posture for as long as you comfortably can, all the while breathing regularly.

**BELOW** *If you can't manage to put both hands on the mat, rest your right arm on your left leg as you twist round.*

### HELPFUL HINTS

Twist your body to the right

Raise your right knee

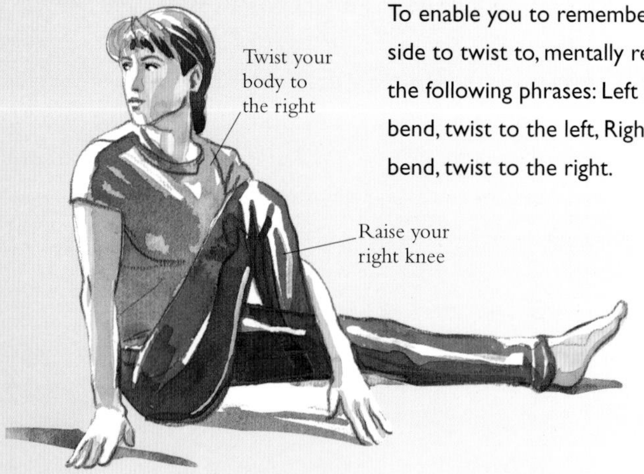

To enable you to remember which side to twist to, mentally repeat the following phrases: Left knee bend, twist to the left, Right knee bend, twist to the right.

**5** Slowly and carefully untwist your body and resume your starting position. Rest briefly.
**6** Repeat the twist to the other side: follow steps 2–5, substituting "right" for "left," and vice versa, in the instructions.

## LATERAL STRETCH

This sideways bending exercise, like the spinal twist, conditions three of the four sets of muscles forming the "abdominal corset." It also exercises the back muscles and so promotes spinal health. In addition, the lateral stretch discourages a build-up of fat at the midriff, and it facilitates deep breathing.

**1** Stand up straight, with your feet fairly close together and your weight equally distributed. Relax your arms at your sides and breathe regularly through your nostrils.

**2** Inhale and raise your arms straight overhead. Press your palms together if you can.

**3** Exhale and bend sideways. Do so slowly and smoothly until your body forms a graceful arch. Keep your upper shoulder back and your arms alongside your ears to ensure a lateral (sideways) rather than a forward bend. (Looking toward your upper arms is also helpful.)

**BELOW**
*Repeat this exercise on both sides to stretch both sets of muscles.*

**4** Maintain this posture for as long as you comfortably can, breathing regularly at all times.

**5** Return to your starting position and then rest.

**6** Now repeat steps 2–5, but this time bend your body in the opposite direction.

Keep your arms alongside your ears

Bend so that you form a graceful arch

### COOLING DOWN

Cooling down after exercising is extremely important. It allows time for static muscle stretching, which enhances your body's overall flexibility. This will prevent any muscle soreness from occuring during the following day. It helps your heart and blood vessels to return gradually to normal functioning and prevents problems related to a sudden drop in blood pressure, such as dizziness and a feeling of light-headedness. Cooling down also facilitates the elimination of metabolic wastes and the replenishing of energy reserves. With the exception of the rock-and-roll exercise in the warm-ups, all the exercises on pages 34–35 can also be used for cooling down. They should be performed slowly, smoothly, and with awareness, and also in synchronization with regular breathing. You may, if you wish, at the end of your exercise session, practice complete relaxation (see *page 56*).

# 4 BREATHWORK

BREATHING IS ALMOST SYNONYMOUS WITH LIFE BECAUSE, IN ONE WAY OR ANOTHER, IT SUPPORTS ALL VITAL FUNCTIONS. YET WE TEND TO IGNORE IT UNTIL WE EXPERIENCE DIFFICULTY WITH IT. BREATHING IS THE KEY INGREDIENT IN BOTH PHYSICAL AND MENTAL HEALTH, AND IT IS THE ONLY FUNCTION THAT CAN BE PERFORMED BOTH INVOLUNTARILY AND VOLUNTARILY. A GREAT DEAL OF ILLNESS ARISES BECAUSE OF NERVOUS SYSTEM IMBALANCES. WORKING ON BREATHING TECHNIQUES CAN SET RIGHT SUCH CHANGES IN EQUILIBRIUM AND WILL BENEFIT MANY VOLUNTARY FUNCTIONS.

## THE RESPIRATORY SYSTEM

We know that we are breathing because we are living. But many of us are not truly alive in the sense that, much of the time, we are not as alert, energetic, productive, and happy as we would like to be. One reason may be that most of us breathe shallowly: inhaled air seldom reaches the bottom of the lungs where the exchange of carbon dioxide for oxygen occurs. It is only when we habitually practice the art of conscious, efficient breathing that we can experience our full potential for well-being in every aspect of life.

By habitually using the "tool" that you carry everywhere with you (your breath), you can learn to alleviate anxiety and promote calm; cope with difficult emotions and with pain; control fatigue and insomnia; make the best of diminished lung capacity if you suffer from asthma or a chronic respiratory (breathing) disorder; and improve your voice to enhance your professional success. You can do all these things by learning and practicing voluntary controlled respiration.

**LEFT** *Taking a few really deep breaths can calm you and help you relax in stressful situations.*

## RESPIRATORY STRUCTURES

Breathing is controlled by the respiratory center in the brain, although it does not require a conscious effort. Breathing begins with the nose where inhaled air is warmed, moistened, and filtered before it enters into the lungs via the windpipe (trachea). The windpipe divides into two air passages called bronchi, which further divide and subdivide into a bronchial tree, ending in about 300 million air sacs, where an exchange of gases (oxygen and carbon dioxide) takes place.

There are many other structures involved in breathing are:

**The lungs:** two lungs, the principal organs of respiration, are located in the chest with the heart between them. They are cone-shaped, with the apex at the top and the broad base at the bottom. Each lung is divided into lobes. These are further divided into lobules into which a small bronchial tube and its terminal air sacs enter. The primary purpose of the lungs is to bring air and blood together in the air sacs so that oxygen can be transmitted to the circulation and carbon dioxide removed.

Lung – expiration

Diaphragm – expiration

Position of the lung and diaphragm during inspiration

**ABOVE** *Efficient breathing also depends on the proper functioning of the diaphragm muscle.*

**Blood vessels:** the pulmonary (lung) artery carries oxygen-poor (deoxygenated) blood from the right side of the heart into the lungs for purification. The pulmonary veins return oxygen-rich (oxygenated) blood to the left side of the heart for distribution all over the body.

**Respiratory muscles:** the muscles involved in breathing are the diaphragm, the intercostals (between the ribs), and several other muscles in the neck, shoulders, chest, and back.

**The diaphragm:** considered the chief muscle of inspiration (breathing in), the diaphragm separates the chest and abdominal cavities. The diaphragm is dome-shaped and when you inhale, the dome lowers and this increases the length of the chest cavity. When you exhale, the diaphragm resumes its dome shape.

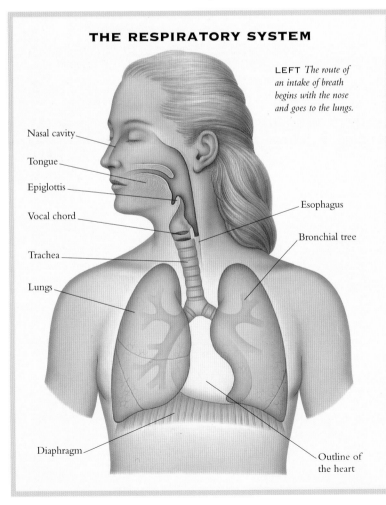

## THE RESPIRATORY SYSTEM

**LEFT** *The route of an intake of breath begins with the nose and goes to the lungs.*

Nasal cavity

Tongue

Epiglottis

Vocal chord

Trachea

Lungs

Diaphragm

Esophagus

Bronchial tree

Outline of the heart

## BREATH AND THE MIND

The ancient practitioners of yoga were probably the first people to discover the intimate relationship between mental states and breathing. This link has now been substantiated by medical scientists. We acknowledge the mind-breath connection in everyday language when we talk about being breathless with excitement; holding our breath in anticipation; a breath-taking spectacle; and getting "second wind" after a period of fatigue.

Changes in emotion are reflected in patterns of breathing, particularly if feelings are intense. Fear, for example, produces fast, shallow breathing. Anger results in short, quick inhalations and strong, rapid exhalations. And in anxiety, breathing tends to be fast and sometimes irregular. Feelings such as joy, love, and forgiveness, by contrast, generate slow, smooth respirations and a general sense of peace and well-being.

**ABOVE** *Yogic breathing is a technique that has to be practiced, but will reap real benefits to physical and mental well-being.*

**ABOVE** *Efficient breathing lifts the spirits and makes you feel much more able to cope with whatever life throws at you.*

Because the relationship between breath and mind is reciprocal, we can alter an emotional state by consciously changing our breathing pattern. When we are stressed or anxious we breathe more rapidly, using only the upper part of the chest. This offers the quickest boost of oxygen to the system, but in the long run is not effective as we are not using the lungs, so waste products build up. Breathing deeply to take in clean air oxygenates the blood and makes the tissue function more efficiently. Air is also thought to have antiseptic properties. Work with mentally ill patients shows that many are shallow breathers, which means that they are depriving themselves of the healing properties of deep breathing.

Learning and practicing unrestricted breathing can help to eliminate painful sensations that are stored deep within us.

Unrestricted breathing promotes relaxation by eliminating certain tensions and inhibitions, and helps suppressed or repressed difficult emotions to come to the surface where they can be examined and then dealt with.

## PREPARING FOR BREATHING EXERCISES

The breathing exercises on pages 44–49 will train you to become more aware of your breathing; to identify unconscious breathing habits that have detracted from healthful living, and to voluntarily replace them with beneficial breathing patterns. Do not expect immediate and dramatic results. Be patient and persevere – your rewards will be proportionate to your efforts.

Before starting the breathing exercises you should take note of the following:

❖ Avoid practicing on a full stomach as it can hinder the free movement of your diaphragm and then the exercises will not be able to be completed properly.

❖ Empty your bladder and even possibly your bowel as well. Make

Hold your head high

Breathe through your nostrils

Relax your jaw and tongue

Relax your rib cage

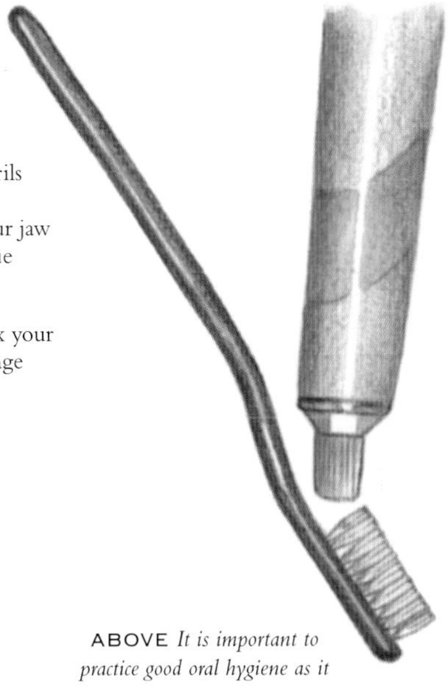

**ABOVE** *It is important to practice good oral hygiene as it can actually help breathing. This is because the mouth is the airway to the lungs.*

sure you clean your teeth and your tongue as the mouth is part of the airways to the lungs.

❖ It is best to choose a stable sitting position and then make sure you maintain good posture. If you decide that you prefer standing, keep your body naturally erect, with the crown of your head uppermost. This will relax your rib cage, prevent compression of your lungs, and facilitate a free flowing of the breath.

❖ Make a quick preliminary body check before starting to exercise and relax any part you find tense. Be sure to relax your jaw and tongue.

❖ Unless otherwise instructed, breathe in and out through your nostrils during the following exercises so that the air will be warmed, moistened, and filtered before it reaches the lungs. Do not, at any time, hold your breath.

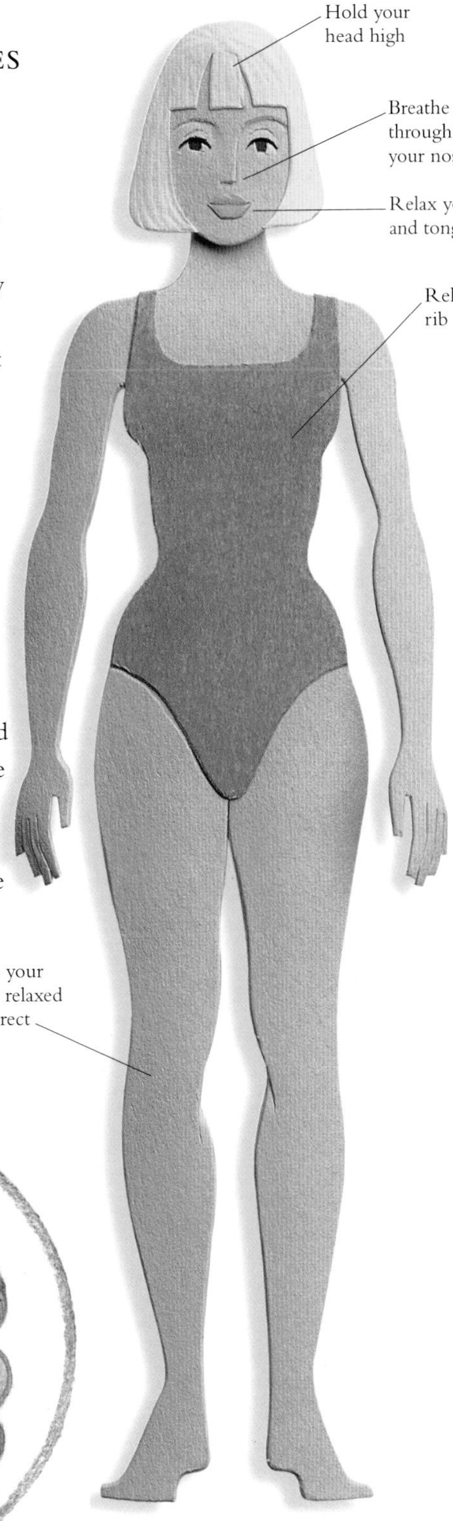

**BELOW** *Breathing exercises cannot be done properly on a full stomach so make sure you eat only lightly before beginning – if at all.*

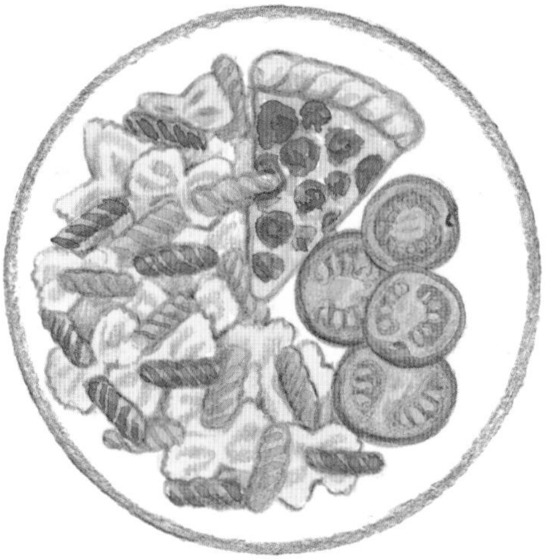

Keep your body relaxed but erect

**ABOVE** *Relax your body and do all you can to ensure that the passage of air is not impeded.*

## ALTERNATE NOSTRIL BREATHING

The two brain hemispheres have different functions: the left chiefly influences language and mathematical skills, while the right controls imaginative and intuitive functions such as spatial orientation and creative thinking. Alternate nostril breathing helps to integrate the functioning of the two brain hemispheres.

Alternate nostril breathing leads to a harmonizing of the body and mind. The exercise is very soothing and relaxing, helping to lessen anxiety, which can aggravate both physical and mental pain. It is also an extremely useful antidote to insomnia.

**1** Sit in any comfortable position and maintain good posture. Breathe regularly.

**2** Rest your left hand in your lap, on your knee, or on the armrest of a chair.

**3** Arrange the fingers of your right hand as follows: fold the two middle fingers toward your palm or rest them lightly on the bridge of your nose; use your thumb to close your right nostril once the exercise is in progress, and your ring finger (or ring and little fingers) to close your left nostril.

**4** Close your eyes (if you wish). Then close your right nostril and inhale slowly, smoothly, and as deeply as you can, without strain, through your left nostril.

**ABOVE** *Find somewhere quiet to practice your breathing. You will feel the benefits of this exercise extremely quickly as it is very relaxing and soothing.*

**5** Close your left nostril and release closure of your right nostril. Exhale.

**6** Then inhale through your right nostril.

**7** Close your right nostril and release closure of your left. Then exhale.

**8** Repeat steps 4–7 as many times as you wish in smooth succession, until you feel an overall sense of calm filling your body.

**9** Relax your right arm and hand. Resume regular breathing. Open your eyes.

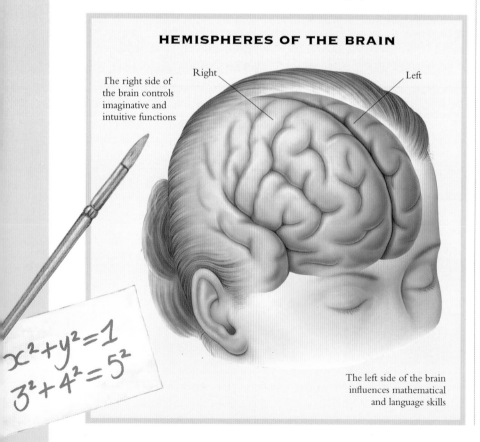

### HEMISPHERES OF THE BRAIN

The right side of the brain controls imaginative and intuitive functions

Right

Left

The left side of the brain influences mathematical and language skills

$$x^2 + y^2 = 1$$
$$3^2 + 4^2 = 5^2$$

**NOTE**

Always switch to the other nostril after inhaling; never after exhaling.

## ANTI-ANXIETY BREATH

This exercise is excellent for counteracting anxiety and averting panic. It is also useful in helping to cope with apprehension, frustration, and anger.

**1** Sit comfortably and maintain good posture. (You may also practice this exercise in a different position if it is more comfortable for you.) Close your eyes or keep them open. Breathe regularly.

**2** Inhale slowly, smoothly, and as deeply as you can without strain.

**3** Exhale slowly, smoothly, and as completely as you can, focusing your attention on your upper abdomen, near your navel.

**4** Before inhaling again, try mentally counting "one thousand," "two thousand." This prolongs the exhalation time and also prevents the overbreathing (hyperventilation) that will sometimes accompany anxiety.

**5** Repeat steps 2–4 again and again in smooth succession, until your breathing has slowed down and you feel calm.

**6** Resume your regular breathing.

## CLEANSING BREATH

Also known as "pursed-lip breathing," this exercise is particularly useful for those with limited lung capacity, such as sufferers of asthma, chronic bronchitis, and emphysema. It prevents the airways from collapsing prematurely, which allows a greater volume of air to be exhaled. You learn to regulate the rate and depth of breathing, and so consciously reduce breathlessness and the feeling of anxiety or panic that often accompanies it.

*BELOW Asthma sufferers might need an inhaler to help them when they are short of breath. However, breathing exercises can help make the most of even limited lung capacity.*

**1** Sit comfortably and maintain good posture. (You may also practice the exercise while lying or standing.) Close your eyes or keep them open. Breathe regularly.

**2** Inhale through your nostrils slowly, smoothly, and as deeply as you can without strain.

Purse your lips

Exhale completely without strain

*ABOVE The breath circulates in through the nose and out through the mouth.*

**3** Purse your lips as if about to whistle or cool a hot drink. Exhale through pursed lips slowly, smoothly, and as completely as possible without strain.

**4** Close your lips but do not clench your teeth; keep your jaw relaxed.

**5** Repeat steps 2–4 as many times as you want to, in a smooth succession.

## COMPLETE BREATH
### (DIAPHRAGMATIC BREATHING)

About 80 percent of breathing is accomplished by the diaphragm. The blood flow at the base of the lungs, close to where the diaphragm is located, is over 2 pints (1 liter) per minute. The blood flow at the top of the lungs, by contrast, is less than one-tenth of that. Yet most of us are utilizing only this area because we tend to breathe shallowly.

ABOVE *The efficiency of the diaphragm can be improved by exercise, just like any other muscle.*

By learning and regularly practicing complete breath (diaphragmatic breathing), you will be able to use your diaphragm more effectively and deeply, with great benefit to your health and well-being. Blood circulation, by which oxygen and nutrients are delivered to all the body's cells, will be improved. Complete breath is also a very important stress management "tool," since it promotes an even flow of breath, which strengthens the nervous system and relaxes the body. It is the most efficient method of breathing as it requires a minimum of effort in return for a maximum intake of oxygen.

Before starting the exercise, you need to locate your diaphragm. In a comfortable sitting, lying (on your back), or standing position, rest your fingers just below your breastbone. Now sniff inward. You will feel the movement of a muscle inside you. This is your diaphragm.

**1** Lie at full length on your back, with a pillow, cushion, or folded towel or blanket under your head. Close your eyes or keep them open. Breathe regularly.

**2** Rest one hand lightly on your abdomen, just beneath your breastbone. Rest the fingers of your other hand on your chest, just below a nipple.

**3** Keeping your abdomen as relaxed as possible, inhale through your nose slowly, smoothly, and as fully as you can without strain. While inhaling, also visualize filling the top, middle, and bottom of your lungs. As you inhale, the hand on the abdomen should rise as the abdomen moves upward. There should be little or no movement of the fingers resting on the chest.

**4** Exhale slowly, smoothly, and as completely as you can while you visualize emptying the top, middle, and bottom of your lungs. As you exhale, the hand on your abdomen should move downward as your abdomen contracts (tightens).

**5** Repeat steps 3 and 4 several times in smooth succession.

**6** Relax your arms and hands. Then rest and try to resume your regular breathing.

BELOW *When you are in a stressful situation, practice your breathing techniques to calm you and help you relax.*

**LEFT** *You can incorporate breathing techniques into everyday activities.*

❖ To help you coordinate inhalation with abdominal relaxation, and exhalation with abdominal contraction, place a lightweight object on your abdomen when first starting to practice complete breath.

❖ Instead of exhaling through your nostrils, you can exhale through pursed lips.

❖ Find ways of incorporating complete breath into your activities of daily living: while waiting for nail polish to dry; while standing in line at the bank, grocery store, or elsewhere; in the doctor's or dentist's waiting-room; or before an interview. No one will know what you are doing.

## HELPFUL HINT

◉ If you feel light-headed at all during this exercise, immediately resume your usual breathing. If you are standing, sit or lie down.

## IT'S LIKE A BALLOON

If you are unsure whether the abdomen should rise or fall, think of a balloon. When you put air into it, it becomes larger; when you let the air out, it becomes flatter. The following phrase may be useful to remember: "Air in, abdomen fat; air out, abdomen flat."

## DIVIDED BREATH

When your chest feels so tight that you cannot take a deep breath in, this is the breathing exercise to choose. Practice it whenever you feel under pressure, to help you to relax and to remain in control.

**1** Sit in any comfortable position and maintain good posture. (You may also practice this exercise while lying down or standing up if you would prefer.)

**2** Take two, three, or more quick inward sniffs, as if breaking up an inhalation into small parts.

**3** Exhale slowly and steadily through your nose or through pursed lips.

*LEFT Wherever you are, taking in short, quick breaths and releasing a long one will loosen your chest and make your breathing easier.*

**4** Repeat steps 2 and 3 several times, until you feel that your chest is relaxing, and until you can take a deep inward breath without straining at all.

### VARIATION

Use the same technique as described in this exercise with your exhalation: divide it into two, three, or more parts of roughly equal length.

## RESPIRATORY CHECKLIST

Keep your body well conditioned. It houses your organs of breathing, and also your circulatory system, which works closely with your respiratory system. The following points form a checklist that you can refer to to ensure you are caring for your respiratory system as well as you can.

⊙ Exercise is good for breathing. Regular practice of the warm-ups and mini-workout on pages 34–37 would be a good starting point.

⊙ Don't smoke. Cigarette smoking is the single most important cause of lung cancer and chronic lung diseases. After smoking a single cigarette, cilia are paralyzed for about an hour and a half. Cilia are hairlike processes lining the airways.

Cilia do a vital job as they propel debris and mucus along, either to be excreted or to be destroyed internally. Repeated smoking can actually permanently damage the cilia, and, as a result, can make the lungs much more vulnerable to infection.

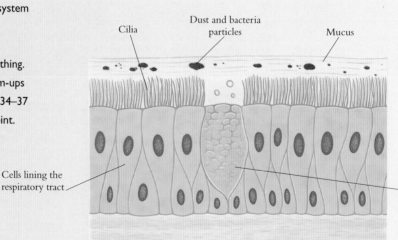

Cilia

Dust and bacteria particles

Mucus

Cells lining the respiratory tract

Goblet cell which secretes mucus

*RIGHT A close-up of a respiratory tract. Today's lifestyle offers many obstacles to a healthy tract – smoking.is the worst.*

## WHISPERING BREATH

If you suffer from asthma or any other disorder that limits your respiratory function, this is a superb exercise to practice. In some respiratory disorders, it is the exhalation phase of breathing that becomes difficult. Practiced regularly, this exercise helps you to gain better control of your exhalation. It also helps to improve your concentration and promote general relaxation.

**1** Sit comfortably in front of a lighted candle. Maintain good posture, relax your hands, and breathe regularly. Keep your eyes open.

**2** Inhale through your nose slowly, smoothly, and as deeply as you can without strain.

**3** Through pursed lips (try pretending you are trying to cool a hot drink and then you will have the right action), blow at the candle flame. Do this slowly, smoothly, gently, and with control. The object of this exercise is to make the flame just flicker; not to put the candle out completely.

**4** Once you have exhaled after doing this, close your mouth but keep your jaw relaxed.

**5** Repeat steps 2–4 several times in smooth succession before resting. After you have done this, resume your regular breathing.

### HELPFUL HINTS

⊙ When you have mastered this exercise, you may dispense with the candle. Instead, close your eyes and blow at an imaginary flame.

⊙ Try practicing the whispering breath while walking up or down the stairs. Keep your eyes open.

AEROSOL PROPELLANTS

PRESERVATIVES IN FOOD

⊙ Practice complete breath every day.

⊙ Look for opportunities to integrate breathing exercises into your daily schedule, such as the ones suggested on page 47.

⊙ Protect yourself from as many respiratory irritants as possible, including aerosols, paints, glues, dust, pollens, animal dandruff, and preservatives in some foods.

PET HAIRS

POLLEN

*RIGHT If you know your breathing is affected by dust, pollen, animal hair, or other irritants, do what you can to avoid them.*

# 5 MINDWORK

WITH THE MOST UP-TO-DATE AND SOPHISTICATED TECHNOLOGY AT THEIR DISPOSAL, RESEARCHERS HAVE NOW BEEN ABLE TO SHOW WITH CERTAINTY THE POWERFUL DEPENDENCE THAT EXISTS BETWEEN THE BODY AND THE MIND. MINDWORK IS ABOUT THE IMPORTANCE OF LEARNING TO USE OUR MENTAL RESOURCES TO ENHANCE BOTH OUR PHYSICAL AND EMOTIONAL WELL-BEING. IT IS CLEAR THAT EXERCISING MENTAL SKILLS SUCH AS CONCENTRATION AND VISUALIZATION CAN STIMULATE A BENEFICIAL PHYSICAL RESPONSE. THE IMPORTANCE OF DEVELOPING THESE TECHNIQUES IS INCREASINGLY BEING RECOGNIZED AS A MEANS OF PROMOTING HEALTH AND WELL-BEING.

## MINDPOWER

Specialists in psychoneuro-immunology (PNI) have cast new light on the mind-body connection. (PNI refers to the interaction among three body systems: endocrine, nervous, and immune.) They have shown that the brain can transmit signals along nerve pathways to reinforce the body's defenses against infection, helping them to put up a fierce fight against disease.

Specialists have also demonstrated that this transmission of nerve signals can be controlled by thoughts and feelings. No longer, therefore, should there be skepticism about results brought about by our own inner, intangible, resources that are unseen to the invisible eye.

**LEFT** *Scientific research has been carried out to show that the way we feel about ourselves affects our physical state as well as our mental state.*

## CONCENTRATION

Although neither visible nor tangible, the human mind is no less real than any organ that can be dissected and tested. Moreover, its resources are vast and still largely untapped. Nevertheless, we have access to a number of mental resources that we can use to our advantage to improve the quality of our life. These include the ability to concentrate, a practice that has become more difficult in an era when innumerable stimuli are constantly competing for our attention.

To conserve energy, to be productive, and to savor the resulting benefits, we need to be able to be very focused, or "one-pointed." The tree exercise shown here on the right and the concentration of sound exercise on page 52 offer a start toward mastering this art.

### HELPFUL HINTS

If you find the Tree Exercise difficult and find that trying to keep your balance takes all your concentration, here are some hints for you to try:

⊙ To help you to establish and maintain your balance, fix your gaze on a still object that is directly in front of you, such as a door handle, an ornament, or a picture on a wall.

⊙ You may also try focusing your attention on your slow, smooth breathing to help to keep you steady.

## THE TREE

This balancing exercise is an excellent exercise for developing nerve-muscle coordination as well as for promoting stillness and concentration.

**1** Stand tall, with your feet together and your arms relaxed at your sides. Keep your eyes open and breathe regularly.

**2** Shift your weight onto one foot. Use your hands to help you to place the sole of your other foot against the inside of the opposite thigh, as high up as you find comfortable.

**3** Inhale and stretch your arms straight overhead; press your palms together if you can.

**4** Stay in this position as long as you comfortably can, and breathe regularly.

**5** Resume your starting position and then rest.

**6** Repeat steps 2–5, but this time balance yourself on your other foot.

## VARIATIONS

❖ Stretch your arms out sideways, at about shoulder level. Relax your wrists.

❖ Try varying your leg position as follows: fold one leg inward, and use your hands to help you to rest the foot carefully against the front of the opposite thigh, as high up as you find comfortable.

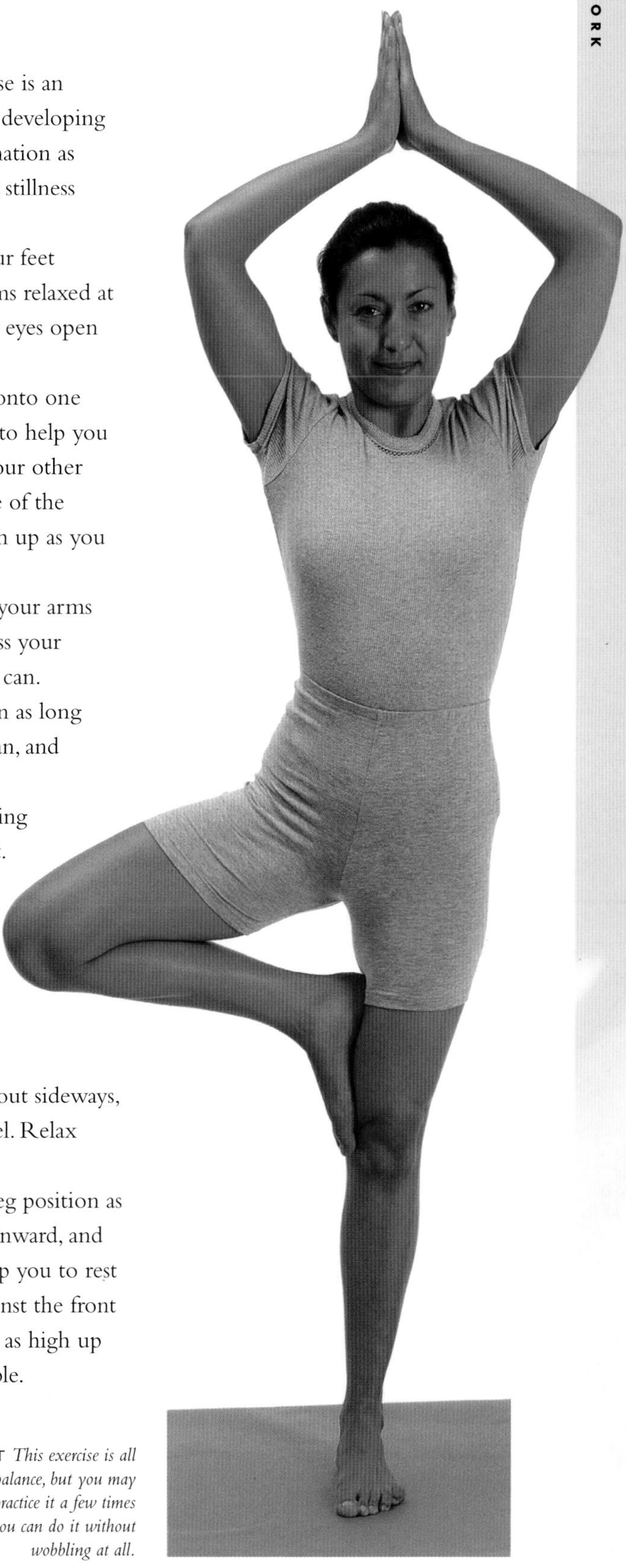

**LEFT** *This exercise is all about balance, but you may have to practice it a few times before you can do it without wobbling at all.*

## CONCENTRATION OF SOUND

### (HUMMING BREATH)

Sounds can have a powerful effect on your state of mind. The most basic of sounds is humming, which is very peaceful. Humming is found, with variation, in virtually every different culture and religious tradition, as part of prayers or meditation rituals. Repeating this sound not only focuses your awareness, but it also promotes a sense of calm.

This exercise focuses on the importance of humming.

1 Begin by sitting in a comfortable position. Relax your hands. Close your eyes and breathe regularly.

2 Inhale air through your nose slowly, smoothly, and as deeply as you possibly can without straining.

3 Then, as you exhale through your nose, again as slowly and smoothly as possible, make a humming sound, like that of a bee. Let the humming last as long as your exhalation does.

4 Repeat steps 2 and 3 in smooth succession as many times as you wish. Keep your attention fully focused on both the breathing process and the humming. Become immersed in the sound. If your attention strays, gently guide it back to the exercise.

5 Resume regular breathing to finish the exercise.

## VISUALIZATION

The ability to form pictures in your mind is known as visualization or imagery. It is not merely wishful thinking, and there is nothing magical about it. Visualization is active and purposeful, and the body is very responsive to it.

In the past couple of decades, researchers have begun to discover that almost anyone can learn to control functions that were formerly thought to be involuntary, such as heart rate, blood pressure, and blood flow to certain parts of the body. When you visualize certain physical changes you wish to take place, they do actually tend to occur, although you may be unaware of the underlying mechanisms. Some people have even used visualization as an adjunct to orthodox therapies to bring themselves into remission from cancer, so it is worth learning the visualization technique for use in your day to day life.

LEFT *Humming is an important part of meditation in many worldwide religions. Here a group of Buddhists are involved in their own meditation ritual.*

## A HEALING VISUALIZATION

This is a simple exercise to learn visualization. Before starting:

❖ Choose a quiet place where you will be able to have about 20 uninterrupted minutes.

❖ Sit or lie comfortably.

❖ Make a quick mental check of your body and relax any part you find tense.

❖ Close your eyes and make sure you breathe regularly.

1 Mentally transport yourself to a place that has pleasant associations for you: a beautiful garden or a quiet beach. Spend a few moments dwelling on details such as the wonderful colors of sea and sky; a gentle breeze caressing your face; the subtle fragrance of flowers; or the taste of salt spray on your lips.

2 With each slow, smooth, deep inhalation, breathe in the healthy fresh air and the untainted smells of this place of retreat.

3 With each unhurried exhalation, let your body sink more deeply into the surface you are sitting or lying on and completely let go of residual tension. Visualize sending away any fatigue you feel or any troubling thoughts, such as those of frustration, anxiety, resentment, or the hurt of rejection.

4 Repeat steps 2 and 3 again and again until you feel calm and comforted, and part of the serene spot you have revisited in thought.

**ABOVE** *The rhythmic flow of the tide can be very soothing. Think of this if you focus on the image of a beach.*

5 When you are ready to return to your usual residence and activities, do so slowly and with awareness, avoiding any jerky movements.

**BELOW** *Focus on the colors of your special garden to heighten the pleasant memories it stirs.*

## MEDITATION

Meditation is a natural device for relaxing your conscious mind without dulling your awareness. Doctors refer to the meditative state as one of "restful alertness," which seems to be an apparent contradiction.

**ABOVE** *Meditation will slow down your heart rate so that it is similar to when you are asleep. This will help you to relax deeply.*

When you are asleep, your heart rate slows down, oxygen consumption decreases, and consciousness fades. When you are awake, by contrast, your heart rate quickens, oxygen consumption increases, and you are usually alert.

These opposites are united in meditation, so that although your body becomes deeply relaxed, you are still conscious and your mind is clear. In essence, then, meditation is a process for quieting the mind and promoting a sense of peace.

### BENEFITS OF MEDITATION

❖ Meditation trains and tunes the mind. The end result is efficiency in daily living.

❖ Because of the many physiological benefits that occur during meditation, and the resulting deep relaxation, inhibitions are shed and any painful feelings that have been repressed or suppressed can rise to the surface and be dealt with. The consequences include greater self-esteem and self-confidence and enhanced productivity.

❖ States such as anxiety, worry, and depression represent concerns about past and future events. Regular meditation helps you take your mind of these things, to live life with full focus on the present.

❖ Researchers contend that long-term meditation helps to keep you young and give some protection against disorders such as heart disease and cancer. In fact, some doctors are recommending one or two periods of daily meditation as an adjunct to treatments for conditions such as high blood pressure, migraine headaches, and stomach ulcers.

Running a home

Supporting a husband

Caring for a family

Taking up outside employment

Shopping and cooking

**LEFT** *Meditation can be used to relax you even when you are doing everyday activities such as walking to work.*

**RIGHT** *With a clear mind you will be better able to juggle the daily routine with which so many women have to contend.*

## A SIMPLE MEDITATION

There are a few things that you should do before starting to practice this meditation technique:

❖ Choose a quiet place where you will have about 20 uninterrupted minutes to do this exercise.

❖ Sit comfortably, and maintain good posture.

❖ Make a quick mental check of your body and relax any part you find tense (*see complete relaxation on page 56*).

❖ Close your eyes and then breathe regularly.

**1** Inhale slowly and smoothly through your nostrils.

**2** As you exhale slowly and smoothly through your nostrils, mentally say to yourself the word "one."

**3** Repeat steps 1 and 2 again and again, over and over in smooth succession.

If your thoughts stray while you are doing this meditation, gently guide them back patiently to both your breathing and the repetition of "one." Do not be discouraged if at first this straying occurs quite frequently. With regular practice, your ability to stay focused will definitely improve.

When you are ready to end your period of meditation, do so slowly; open your eyes and then gently stretch your limbs. Never come out of meditation suddenly, but rather take your time over it or you will immediately lose the benefits you have gained from practicing this meditation.

RIGHT *Wear loose clothing, make sure the temperature is comfortable, and try to ensure you will not be disturbed.*

### HELPFUL HINTS

⊙ You may start with 5–10 minutes of meditation daily and gradually increase this to 20 minutes twice daily.

⊙ Meditate before a meal, never after, to avoid the process of digestion from interfering with your concentration.

⊙ Substitute any word or phrase for "one." Particularly effective is something related to your religion or belief system. Suggestions include: peace, love, relax, I feel calm.

## COMPLETE RELAXATION

True relaxation is not a matter of collapsing on a couch with a drink. Deep and complete relaxation is a nerve-muscle (neuromuscular) skill that needs to be learned. The technique below provides training in this skill; time, effort, and patience invested in its regular practice will bring invaluable benefits. Keep a sweater or blanket and a pair of socks nearby. Use them to prevent you from becoming cold as your body cools down.

**STEP 1**

1 Lie at full length on your back on your mat. Separate your legs. Relax your arms a little away from your side; turn your palms upward. Position your head for maximum comfort. Close your eyes and breathe regularly.

2 Push your heels away from you. Note the resulting stiffness that you can feel in your legs. Maintain this tension (from now on, referred to as "hold") for a few seconds, without holding your breath.

**LEFT** *Before you start this relaxation exercise, do ensure that you have a blanket and pair of socks nearby in case you become cold.*

3 Let go of the stiffness in your legs. Relax them. Relax your feet. (From now on, this letting go of tension is referred to as "release.")

4 Tighten your buttocks. Hold. Release. Relax your hips.

5 Exhale and press the small of your back (waist) toward or against the mat. Feel your abdominal muscles tighten. Hold as long as your exhalation lasts. Release as you inhale. Relax your back and your abdomen.

6 Inhale and squeeze your shoulder blades together. Hold. Release as you exhale.

7 Shrug your shoulders as if to touch your ears with them. Hold. Release. Relax your shoulders.

### BENEFITS OF RELAXATION

This Complete Relaxation exercise has many benefits for your body. It:

⊙ Eliminates all the unnecessary tension that can be found all over the body.

⊙ Keeps blood pressure within normal limits.

⊙ Promotes sound, refreshing sleep when it is done just before bedtime.

⊙ Conserves energy and prevents fatigue.

⊙ Promotes poise and vitality.

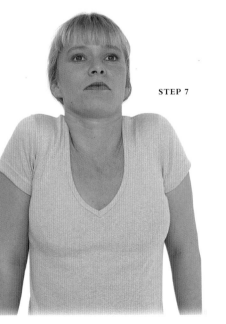

**STEP 7**

**STEP 9**

8 Carefully tilt your head slightly backward. Feel the resulting gentle stretching of the front of your neck. Hold this tilt. Then release. Now carefully reposition your head back to the upright position. Relax your throat.

9 Carefully tilt your head forward, tucking in your chin.
Feel the gentle stretch of the back of your neck this time. Again, hold this stretch. Now release. Carefully reposition your head upright before relaxing your neck once more.

10 Raise your eyebrows to form horizontal wrinkles on your forehead. Hold. Release. Relax your brow.

11 Squeeze your eyes shut. Hold. Release. Relax your eyes.

12 Exhaling, open your mouth wide. Stick out your tongue; open your eyes as if staring; tighten all the muscles of your face and throat. Hold the facial tension as long as your exhalation lasts. Inhale, pull in your tongue, close your mouth and eyes, and relax your throat and facial muscles. Breathe regularly.

13 Stiffen and raise your arms off the mat. Make fists. Hold. Release. Relax your arms and hands. Let them rest with their full weight on the mat.

14 Now direct your awareness to your breathing. Observe the slow rhythm of the breath. With each inhalation, visualize filling your system with positive forces such as love, joy, hope, and forgiveness. With each exhalation, imagine sending away troubling emotions such as pessimism and anger, and let your body sink more deeply into the mat.

End your relaxation slowly and with awareness. Stretch your limbs, carefully roll your head from side to side and make any other gentle movements you feel the urge to do. Roll onto your side and use your hands to help you to sit up.

## HELPFUL HINTS

Start with a daily session of about 10 minutes of step-by-step Complete Relaxation, as described. A good time to practice this, if it is at all possible, is straight after you come home from work and before you start your household chores. Alternatively, you may want to integrate it into your coffee or lunch break at work, to help you counteract fatigue during your working day. Try it also before bedtime, to promote calm and sound sleep. As you become used to the technique, gradually increase the total relaxation time up to 20 or 30 minutes.

STEP 13

STEP 10

STEP 12

## LISTENING
## TO SILENCE

**M**any of us seem to need an almost constant companion in the form of sound, be it the small-talk of acquaintances or music on the radio as we drive along. We seem ill at ease when alone, surrounded by silence, and yet silence is just as necessary to our well-being as sound is. One balances the other to produce a natural harmony without which various forms of malaise arise.

Researchers have noted, for example, that loud music, listened to in confined spaces such as in motor vehicles while traveling long distances, raises blood pressure. Done habitually, this could conceivably place an undue strain on the heart with unhappy consequences.

To be whole and to remain whole, or integrated, we need to avail ourselves of counterirritants to the potentially harmful effects of the continual noise assaulting our sense of hearing. There is no better antidote than taking time out to listen to the calming sounds of silence.

In every disciplined life, time is set aside for silence. Nuns and monks spend periods of time when not a word passes their lips. Because they expend less energy through speech, they conserve more of it for themselves and for their service to others.

To those who know how to listen, silence does indeed speak: of joy and sorrow; of things accomplished and of those left undone; of paths to tread and of those to leave untried. It never tells us what we want to hear simply because we expect it. Instead, it expresses what we need to know: simple, unbiased truths, like why we feel neglected or rejected; unfulfilled or alone. But we must first learn to be still and to listen with understanding while the silence speaks to us.

The most effective preparation for this is daily meditation (*see page 54*). Meditating daily will train you to be alone without being lonely, and quiet without feeling anxious.

As you learn how to be still, you will find self-observation becoming easier than it was before. You will better be able to identify any physical and psychological warning signs, such as those of fatigue or depression, and will then be able to heed them before they become

**LEFT** *Take time out of your busy schedule to be still and listen to the calming influence of silence. You will find you will reap benefits from this.*

**ABOVE** *Don't mistake being alone for loneliness. Enjoy your own company and savor some quiet contemplation.*

unmanageable. You will be better able to reflect on questions to which you need honest answers and will find that responses occur more clearly than if you were surrounded by distractions in the form of people and things. You will, in time, experience self-healing and a sense of self-fulfilment in the silence. For it is only when we are quiet that we can find the answers that often escape us amid the hustle and bustle of everyday activity.

## SOMETHING TO TRY

On your next camping trip or excursion into the country, try taking a tape recorder with you and then record nature's sounds at dusk or daybreak: a squirrel scurrying up a tree or shuffling through leaves looking for something to eat; a bird calling to its mate in the distance; water rushing; rain pitter-pattering on the top of a tent; pine trees whispering; or even fish jumping.

Once you have your recording, retreat somewhere alone and play back the tape. Savor each one of the sounds you captured. You will find this relaxing and uplifting.

**RIGHT** *Record the uplifting sounds of nature to raise your spirits.*

# 6 SEXUALITY

REGARDLESS OF HER AGE, SIZE, APPEARANCE, OR SOCIAL STATUS, EVERY WOMAN'S SEXUALITY DESERVES RESPECT. A WOMAN'S SEXUALITY IS INTIMATELY CONNECTED NOT ONLY TO HER RELATIONSHIP WITH HER PARTNER, BUT TO HER RELATIONSHIP WITH HERSELF AND, INDEED, THE WORLD AROUND HER. WOMEN PLACE GREAT VALUE ON FORMS OF EMOTIONAL COMMUNICATION OTHER THAN SEXUAL INTERCOURSE ITSELF. KNOWING THAT THEY ARE LOVED AND CARED FOR PROVIDES THE REASSURANCE THEY NEED TO FEEL SECURE IN A RELATIONSHIP. THEY DO NOT DISMISS THE FULFILMENT DERIVED FROM THE SEX ACT, BUT SEE SEXUALITY AS A WHOLE-PERSON FUNCTION INVOLVING BOTH BODY AND MIND.

## COMMUNICATION

Many of the problems that arise in women's relationship with men can be traced to differences in their styles of communication. Women tend to process emotional information faster than men, and to react more quickly and spontaneously. This is particularly true of extrovert women. The problem with this is that it may be seen by the male as pressure to respond when he hasn't had enough time to receive and process the information.

Men, by comparison, find it difficult to process their thoughts quickly enough to translate them into sensitively phrased sentences. They seem to need a period of time in which to examine a situation factually and logically before making a response.

**ABOVE** *The difference in the emotional response to circumstances is one of the main causes of communication breakdown between the sexes.*

This delay may be perceived by the woman as a lack of caring.

Both men and women tend to believe that they do give a great deal but do not receive proportional return. They often perceive that the love they give is inadequately acknowledged and appreciated. Communication experts assert, however, that both in fact give love but not in the way the other desires.

## DIFFERENT NEEDS

All human beings have, on the whole, the same basic needs. Apparently more important to women, however, is the need to feel that they are being cared for, understood, respected, and considered worthy, and they also need to be reassured. Women need to be aware that, by comparison, men primarily need to feel trusted, accepted, appreciated, admired, and encouraged.

When a woman perceives that her partner is inattentive and therefore uninterested in what she is saying, she feels unloved. When she believes that he is putting work and his time with friends before her and their children, she feels unimportant. When she is upset and he appears to minimize it, she feels unsupported. And when he gives her the silent treatment in response to her expressed feelings, instead of receiving the reassurance she seeks, she at once feels insecure.

On the other hand, when a woman emphasizes the omissions, rather than the things her male partner has done for her, he feels unappreciated. When she tells him how to do something or corrects his behavior, he feels that she does not admire him. When she chides him for an apparent wrong, he feels a lack of approval. And when she criticizes him or takes initiative away from him, he feels discouraged.

## UNDERSTANDING EACH OTHER'S NEEDS

When relationships become difficult, people tend to give up. When they begin to understand each other's needs, however, relationships become easier. But people need to talk to each other and to really listen to each other, in a non-judgmental way, in order to find out what these needs are.

Some couples find counseling useful in helping to identify and to resolve communication problems. The counselor is a disinterested professional and the information shared is confidential. There are also books available on both communication and listening skills. It would be well worthwhile looking at a few *(see bibliography, page 126).*

Enlisting a partner's cooperation may require a great deal of creativity and may be quite a challenge to your communications skills. The following tips will hopefully help you as you try to improve your relationship:

❖ Learn to share your feelings with him in a forthright but sensitive way.

❖ Don't ask him too many questions when he is upset; give him time.

❖ Don't give him a lecture, criticize him, or try to improve him yourself.

❖ Don't offer him unsolicited advice. It will not be appreciated.

❖ Don't expect him to match every sacrifice you make with one of his own.

❖ Learn to be independent without making him feel that he is not needed.

**BELOW** *Talking to a neutral third party can help resolve problems and clear the air when the situation is tense between partners.*

**RIGHT** *Even the most loving couples experience some sexual problems at times. Don't be afraid to talk about your feelings and needs.*

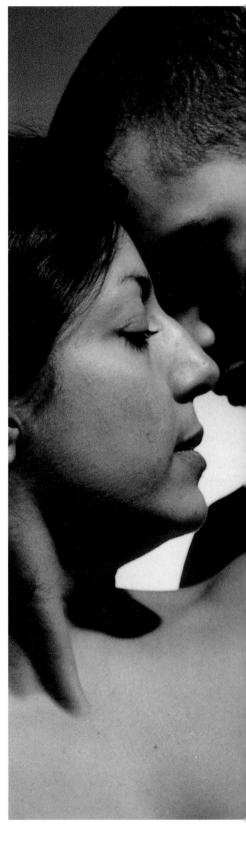

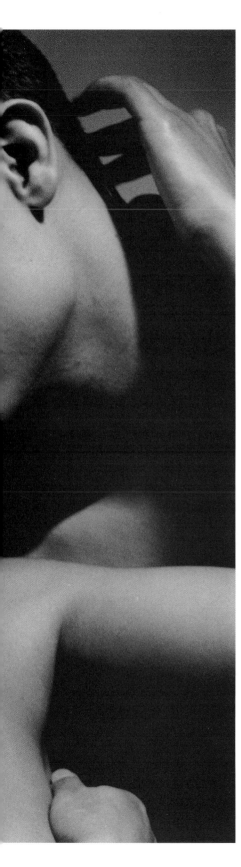

## SEXUAL PROBLEMS

Western societies tend to overrate sexual performance. This generates a great deal of anxiety, which in turn undermines the quality of intimate relationships. Also, when partners have different degrees of sexual appetite, it is often perceived as a major problem rather than a difference in temperament. When both women and men, however, are freed from the pressures to perform sexually, they are much more likely to discover other equally meaningful forms of intimacy, and be motivated to practice them.

Among the sexual problems women experience, lack of desire (whether continuous or sporadic) is perhaps the most widespread. Common too is the failure to experience orgasm. Causes include: physical and environmental factors and attributes; some medications, alcohol consumption, and drug abuse; and hormonal cycles.

Some women's interest in sex declines after surgical removal of an ovary. In addition to producing the female hormone, estrogen, ovaries also produce the male hormone, testosterone, which is responsible for libido (the sex urge). Estrogen replacement

**ABOVE** *Physical love is just one aspect of a relationship that fulfils both spiritual and psychological needs.*

alone may not therefore be sufficient to restore interest in sex.

Some medications prevent spontaneity and enjoyment in sexual relations, and also the ability to experience orgasm. Notable are some of the antidepressants, neuroleptics (anti-psychotics), and medications used to lower blood pressure. Oral contraceptives are also known to depress libido.

Another deterrent to satisfying sex is inadequate vaginal lubrication. This could be caused by a deficiency of estrogen or by disorders such as diabetes. It may also be the result of fear, anxiety, and high stress levels. Women being investigated for infertility, for example, can become so highly anxious that they fail to enjoy sex. Painful intercourse (dyspareunia) may be a consequence of conditions such as pelvic inflammatory disease (PID), bladder infection, and endometriosis. (The latter is when the lining of the uterus appears in areas other than the uterus. It is thought to be caused by fragments of the lining that are shed during menstruation traveling up the fallopian tubes to the pelvic cavity. They continue to respond to the menstrual cycle and bleed each month, but the blood is trapped, causing cysts.)

## SEXUALLY TRANSMITTED DISEASES

Women's sexuality cannot be discussed without mention of sexually transmitted diseases (STDs) because of their impact on reproductive life and also because of the ill effects of disease on the unborn child. This impact takes various forms, including pelvic inflammatory disease (PID), infertility, ectopic pregnancy (pregnancy outside of the uterus), and miscarriage. STDs have become a major health concern. There are more than 50 STDs, of which eight are potentially fatal. The "big eight" are: (human immunodeficiency virus) HIV/(acquired immune deficiency syndrome) AIDS, hepatitis B and C, genital warts or HPV (human papilloma virus), genital herpes, chlamydia, gonorrhea, and syphilis.

*RIGHT If you notice any changes in your body, consult your doctor or health professional for an early diagnosis and peace of mind.*

Women can help to protect themselves against STDs by becoming informed, obtaining appropriate testing (screening), and by building the self-esteem and acquiring the skills necessary to gain their partners' cooperation in practicing safe sex.

*BELOW Barrier methods of contraception also help prevent the spread of sexually transmitted diseases.*

### HELPFUL HINT

If you have any concerns or questions about your health at all, do consult your doctor or other health professional. There are STD clinics, and testing can be anonymous. Treatment in many cases is fairly straightforward, and the confidentiality of the patient is always honored.

### HIV/AIDS

HIV/AIDS is generally transmitted by having sexual intercourse with an HIV-positive partner or from infected blood, usually from sharing HIV-contaminated needles. The sharing of needles used to inject steroids for body-building, and contaminated needles used during tattooing (body art) can also pose a risk. There is as yet no cure but courses of antiviral drugs help to alleviate symptoms.

### HEPATITIS B AND C

These are transmitted mainly through sexual intercourse. They can be fatal in their acute stage, but most people can overcome the viruses. Some people become carriers of the disease and, although they are well themselves, they can pass the organisms to sexual partners. There is no specific treatment for any viral hepatitis, although there is a vaccine for hepatitis B.

## GENITAL WARTS

Genital warts are caused by the human papillomar virus (HPV). The virus is normally transmitted by sexual contact. Typically, the warts occur in multiple, painless clusters on the vulva, vagina, cervix, perineum, anorectal area, and the urethral opening one to two months after exposure. Lesions (diseased parts) can also occur in the mouth, pharynx, and the larynx. HPV can cause infection of the larynx in infants born to mothers with vaginal warts. HPV is also a risk factor in cervical cancer (see page 113).

Genital warts can be treated by a doctor, without pain, while they are small. Left untreated, however, they may need to be removed surgically. Untreated, they increase the risk of cancers of the reproductive organs. It is important for sexually active women to have regular cervical smears (tests done for the early detection of cancer cells, especially in the cervix and vagina).

## GENITAL HERPES

The genital herpes virus is similar to the herpes virus that causes the common cold sore on the lips. One mode of transmission is oral sex. The offending organisms can be dormant in the body for many years. A baby born to a woman with genital herpes may become very ill. To avoid this possibility, a Caesarean section may be necessary.

Genital herpes can be treated with antiviral drugs and pain-killers, as well as bathing in salt water.

**ABOVE** *STDs can affect the unborn child, so women in high-risk groups need to be aware of the implications if they plan to conceive.*

## CHLAMYDIA AND GONORRHEA

These are dubbed "the silent disease'" because most people infected with them are free of symptoms. Chlamydia and gonorrhea are rarely fatal in men, but they can be lethal in women, if left untreated. The causative organisms can move upward from the vagina and infect the entire reproductive system. They can then enter the abdominal cavity and cause PID.

Both diseases are treated with a course of antibiotics.

## SYPHILIS

Syphilis is an infectious, chronic venereal disease characterized by lesions (local diseased parts) that may involve any tissue or organ. The causative organism (Treponema pallidum) is transmitted by direct contact between humans with freshly contaminated material, transfusion of infected blood, or from a pregnant woman to her unborn child. It can also enter the body through a break in the skin or mucous membrane. Syphilis is treated with penicillin.

**BELOW** *The perceived stigma of contracting an STD should not deter you from seeking treatment as soon as possible.*

## CONTRACEPTION

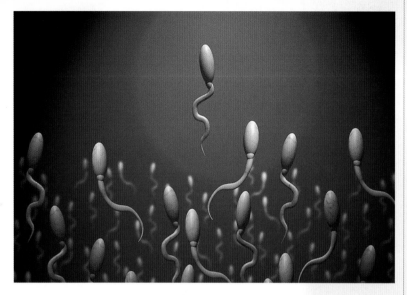

ABOVE *Use a barrier method of contraception to prevent sperm coming in contact with the egg.*

Contraception is the prevention of conception, the union of the male sperm and the female egg (ovum). A contraceptive is any process, device, or method that is used by a couple to prevent contraception. Contraceptives fall into the following categories: steroids; chemical; physical or barrier; combinations of physical or barrier and chemical; natural; and permanent.

### STEROIDS
Steroids work by disrupting the body's normal balance of hormones so that an egg is not released at all.
**Oral contraceptives:** commonly known as "the pill." They are composed of chemicals that are similar to natural hormones (estrogen and progesterone), and they act by preventing ovulation. When taken according to instructions, they are nearly 100 percent effective.

**Long-acting injectable or implanted steroid contraceptives:** this method of contraceptive is still undergoing clinical trials. It is injected into the muscle and gradually released into the bloodstream over three months and is a highly effective method.

**Diethylstibestrol:** used as a "morning after" contraceptive, especially in cases of rape or incest.

### CHEMICAL
This method actually kills any sperm it comes into contact with.
**Spermicides:** agents that kill sperm; cream, foam, jelly, spermicide-impregnated sponge, or suppositories are placed in the vagina prior to intercourse. They may be used alone or in combination with a barrier contraceptive such as a diaphragm. Their effectiveness is moderate to good, depending on proper use.

### PHYSICAL OR BARRIER
In physical methods devices are placed so that the fertilized egg cannot implant itself on the womb. This is very effective. In barrier methods sperm is prevented from reaching the egg by a barrier that is placed in the way. Again, this is effective.

LEFT *Contraceptives can be steroids, chemical, physical, barrier, natural, or permanent.*

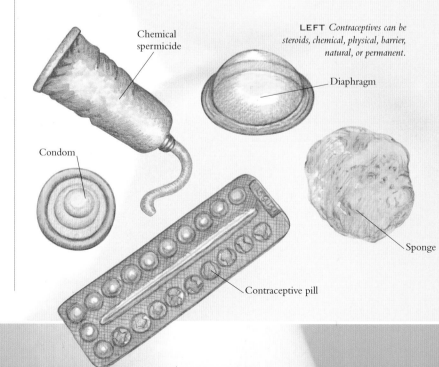

Chemical spermicide

Diaphragm

Condom

Sponge

Contraceptive pill

**Intra-uterine contraceptive device (IUD):** also known as a coil or loop, this is a plastic or metal device that is placed inside the uterus. It is thought to act as a contraceptive by preventing the fertilized egg from attaching itself to the lining of the uterus. The effectiveness of this method is considered slightly lower than that of oral contraceptives.

**Diaphragm:** a dome-shaped piece of rubber with a flexible spring around the edge, also known as a cap. It is inserted into the vagina to cover the cervix. In order for it to be effective, it must be used with a chemical spermicide, which should be applied prior to inserting the diaphragm. A cervical cap is a smaller version.

**Sponge:** this is impregnated with a contraceptive cream or jelly and has to be inserted into the vagina several hours before intercourse.

**Condom:** this method is used by a male partner. It is a flexible tube-shaped barrier that is placed over the penis to contain the ejaculate so that it is not deposited into the vagina. Used properly, condoms are considered a reliable means of contraception, particularly if they are combined with a chemical spermicide.

By providing a physical barrier between the genitals of both partners, condoms help to prevent the spread of STDs.

**Female condom:** this is similar to the male condom but it is larger. It is inserted into the woman's vagina and has rings to hold it in place during intercourse.

**LEFT** *Natural methods of contraception may depend on your menstrual cycle being regular and predictable.*

## NATURAL

No devices or chemicals are used in natural methods, but they are not very reliable.

**Ovulation methods:** these require abstinence from intercourse for a specified number of days before, during, and after ovulation.

The rhythm is based on calculating the fertile period by the calendar. This method, however, has a high failure rate.

Other ovulation methods determine ovulation by charting the woman's basal temperature, or by observing cyclical changes in the cervical mucus.

**Withdrawal:** this is done by the man withdrawing his penis from the vagina just prior to ejaculation. In practice, it has a high failure rate since sperm may also be present in the pre-ejaculatory fluid – therefore a woman still runs the risk of becoming pregnant.

## PERMANENT

This is an irreversible, surgical method to ensure that the woman does not fall pregnant. A drastic but effective method.

**Tubal ligation:** this involves surgical division of the fallopian tubes and tying the cut ends. Effective as a contraceptive method, but it is virtually irreversible. It is also necessary to consider the possible complications of surgery.

**Vasectomy:** this method consists of cutting the man's vas deferens (the tube that transports sperm from testis to urethra) and tying each end so that sperm cannot reach the urethra. It has to be done on both sides and the ejaculate is then tested for several months to be certain that no sperm are present. Attempts to reverse the procedure have been successful in only a small number of cases.

PART TWO

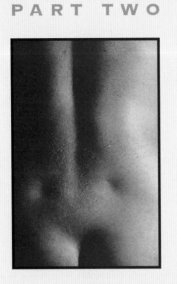

# PROBLEM SOLVING AND SPECIAL CONCERNS

# 7 STRESS MANAGEMENT

STRESS OCCURS WHEN THE DEMANDS OF OUR ENVIRONMENT, EXTERNAL OR INTERNAL, EXCEED OUR RESOURCES FOR COPING WITH THEM. NOTABLE STRESS-PRODUCING AGENTS, OR STRESSORS, INCLUDE ANXIETY, FEAR, UNCERTAINTY, GUILT, FRUSTRATION, CONFLICT, REGRET, AN ACCIDENT, OR THE LOSS OF SOMEONE OR SOMETHING SIGNIFICANT. OTHER STRESSORS TAKE THE FORM OF EVERYDAY ANNOYANCES IN OUR LONG-TERM RELATIONSHIPS WITH OTHERS: A PARTNER, CHILDREN, OR CO-WORKERS. SOME ARE OF SHORT DURATION, BUT THESE ARE USUALLY MORE PRONOUNCED THAN LONGSTANDING STRESSES. ALL CAN DAMAGE OUR HEALTH AND DETRACT FROM THE JOY OF LIVING.

## THE STRESS RESPONSE

Stressors are responsible for a number of physiological adjustments known collectively as the stress response. This response is initiated in a small area of the brain called the hypothalamus, which responds to messages from various organs and controls the body's automatic processes. In any situation that you perceive as threatening, dangerous, or overwhelming, a number of bodily changes take place. Some of them you will be aware of but others are undetected. They include:

❖ Increased pulse rate.
❖ Elevated blood pressure.
❖ Accelerated rate of breathing.
❖ Rigidity of the muscles of the neck and back.
❖ Temporary impairment of digestion.

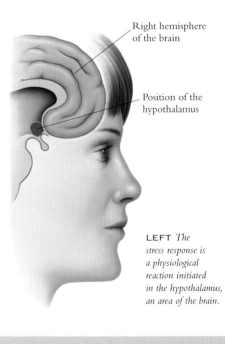

Right hemisphere of the brain

Position of the hypothalamus

LEFT *The stress response is a physiological reaction initiated in the hypothalamus, an area of the brain.*

* Shortened blood-clotting time.
* Withdrawal of mineral from your bones.
* Mobilization of fat from different storage sites.
* Retention of an abnormal amount of salt.

Too many difficult or upsetting life changes, such as the loss of a partner, loss of employment, separation, or divorce and a change of residence, in too short a space of time, causes stress, which then increases our chances of accident or illness.

## STRESS CONTROL STRATEGIES

If you can look at an event or circumstance and view it as something that is not going to last forever, and over which you do have a measure of control, then you have already begun to practice effective stress control. Through self-observation and listening to your body's signals, you can learn to develop a "fine tuning-in" that will alert you to any rising stress levels that may occur. This means that you can then rapidly take the appropriate measures to cope with them. One of the best practices is daily mediation (see page 54).

There are other ways to manage stress effectively:
* Maintaining good health.
* Learn to recognize the symptoms of stress, such as rapid breathing, heart palpitations, irritability, anxiety, diarrhea, headache, or backache.

* Talk about your feelings and problems rather than bottling them up inside you.
* If you are angry, channel the anger constructively: through vigorous exercise such as brisk walking, running, or playing tennis. Speak up if you have a problem. Learn to be assertive but avoid being aggressive.
* Establish and maintain a sound support system. Trusted friends or relatives will provide you with encouragement, counteract your feelings of isolation, and will help to promote a sense of self-worth and confidence.
* If possible, put some distance between yourself and your source of stress to take stock and regain your perspective.
* As an antidote to the possible unpleasant effects of the first few seconds of a stressful situation, smile inwardly as well as with your eyes and mouth. Relax your jaw and slow down your breathing. Mentally tell yourself that you're calm, alert, and in control.
* Learn to laugh. It lights up your face and relaxes your muscles. It also encourages the release of natural pain-killers, boosts the immune system, and forces stale air out of the lungs and fresh air in.
* Love and respect yourself. Low self-esteem is a form of self-rejection, and that is the ultimate stressor.

RIGHT *If you don't learn to manage stressful situations, they can overwhelm you, but there are positive steps you can take.*

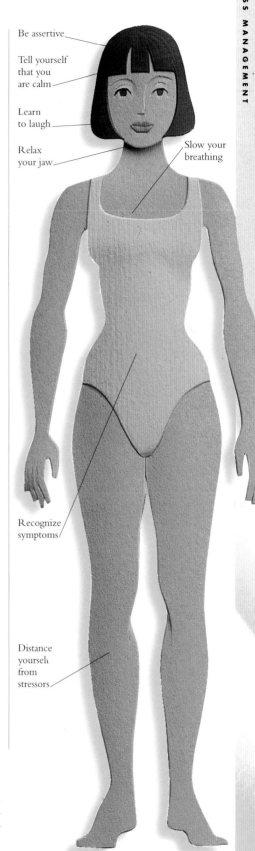

Be assertive

Tell yourself that you are calm

Learn to laugh

Relax your jaw

Slow your breathing

Recognize symptoms

Distance yourself from stressors

# TIME MANAGEMENT

A major cause of stress for many women is not having enough time to do all the things they want and need to do, and the tremendous feeling of pressure this generates. However, when the priorities are identified and a plan of action is devised, certain practices and habits can be modified, resulting in a considerable easing of this feeling of distress. Managing time is, in reality, managing yourself.

**BELOW** *Prioritize your workload. Learn to recognize the difference between urgent and important.*

The secret of being able to do everything, without the frustration of not having enough time, is to work effectively ("work smart") rather than work longer or harder.

## THE BEST USE OF TIME

Avoid wasting time and make the very best of what time is available:

❖ Ailments and illness result in poor productivity. Keep fit *(see caring for yourself, page 14).*

❖ Traveling to and from work and driving children to various activities is time-consuming. If you can't find ways of reducing time

**ABOVE** *Even very young children can learn to shake a pillow or do some dusting. Share out the chores.*

spent commuting, try to find profitable ways of using the time you are commuting (such as listening to an educational cassette).

❖ Clutter detracts from effectiveness. Keep your work areas and surroundings organized.

❖ Doing everything yourself can result in exhaustion and leave you no time for yourself. Learn to delegate chores to your children, partners, and others.

❖ Failure to plan: time given to intelligent planning is well spent. It reduces the time required for the actual project.

❖ An inability to concentrate results in disorganization and forgetfulness, both of which are major time-wasters. Practice

**ABOVE** *It is important to schedule in some "play" time just for you, to ensure balance.*

meditation and concentration techniques regularly to help you to develop the art of keeping focused *(see pages 50–59).*

❖ Inability to say "no" leads to overcommitment. Take a course in assertiveness training to help you to learn how to say "no" graciously and without guilt.

❖ Procrastination is the thief of time. Explore the causes underlying your tendency to delay doing particular things, and then try to find constructive ways of overcoming them.

❖ Striving for perfection is futile. Aim instead for excellence, but don't be too hard on yourself.

❖ Interruptions: protect yourself from unnecessary claims on your time. It's not the time spent on a task that is significant, but rather the amount of uninterrupted time.

Time management experts identify many other time-wasters, and books on the subject give suggestions for dealing with them *(see bibliography on page 126).*

## TIME FOR RELAXATION

Practice some form of relaxation every day. Local relaxation prevents a build-up of tension in individual body parts, such as the jaw, neck, and shoulders. Practicing a general relaxation technique will reduce tension in the entire body *(see pages 56–57).*

Make time for play as well. Balance your work with a sport or hobby – something you enjoy. Play for fun rather than for competition as this will keep stress levels down.

### TIME-WASTERS

Universal time-wasters include:

- Illness
- Clutter
- Commuting
- Doing everything yourself
- Failure to plan
- Poor concentration
- Inability to say "no"
- Procrastination
- Perfectionism
- Interruptions

# 8 MENTAL HEALTH

THE BODY AND MIND ARE INTIMATELY CONNECTED; MENTAL HEALTH DEPENDS ON PHYSICAL WELL-BEING AND VICE VERSA. IN FACT, MENTAL FITNESS MAY BE EVEN MORE IMPORTANT THAN OUR PHYSICAL HEALTH SINCE OUR STATE OF MIND POWERFULLY INFLU-ENCES HOW WE TAKE CARE OF OURSELVES, AND HOW MOTIVATED WE ARE TO DO SO. CARING FOR OTHERS MAY CAUSE US TO NEGLECT OURSELVES AND TO IGNORE BOTH OUR PHYSICAL AND MENTAL WELL-BEING. WE NEED TO BE AWARE OF THE WARNING SIGNS OF MENTAL ILLNESS AND THE NEED TO SEEK PROFESSIONAL HELP. SEEKING HELP IS A SIGN OF STRENGTH, NOT OF WEAKNESS.

## LIFE CRISIS

Certain events are so powerful and so emotionally taxing that they can precipitate a breakdown of mental health. These events include:

❖ The death of a partner, child, or parent.

❖ A serious accident or illness.

❖ Separation from a partner, or divorce.

❖ Loss of employment.

❖ Children leaving home ("empty nest" syndrome).

❖ Retirement from work.

If you are experiencing one or more of these life changes, try not to isolate yourself. Keep in touch with caring friends or family, or join a support group. If these supports are not enough, seek professional help. Above all, do not neglect yourself. Eat well, take regular exercise, preferably in the fresh air, take steps to obtain proper sleep, and try and do some form of relaxation daily *(See Achieving Optimum Well-Being on pages 10–67).*

**LEFT** *Talking to someone who has experienced the crisis you are going through can really help.*

## MYTHS

There are numerous misconceptions about mental illness. These include the belief that:

⊙ Psychiatric problems affect more women than men.

⊙ The chances of depression increase with menopause.

⊙ You are more at risk from depression if you are busy than when you are less busy.

⊙ Mental illness affects only those of low economic status.

⊙ Mentally ill people are violent and dangerous.

⊙ People with mental illness are of low intelligence.

⊙ Mental illness is due to personal weakness.

Seeking information from authoritative sources is the first essential step toward dispelling these myths. Consult your doctor, and read some of the many helpful books *(see bibliography on page 126)*

## ANXIETY

Anxiety is often described as a feeling of nervousness. Psychologists who have tried to distinguish between anxiety and fear say that the latter describes a response to a concrete and immediate danger, whereas with anxiety the sufferer does not seem to know clearly what the danger is, when it will occur, or how it might be dealt with.

**ABOVE** *Even joyous occasions can bring feelings of anxiety, often coupled with guilt.*

### SYMPTOMS

Anxiety manifests itself in a wide variety of ways that include:

❖ Shakiness.

❖ Inability to relax.

❖ Trouble with sleeping.

❖ Loss of appetite.

❖ Breathing difficulty.

❖ Rapid heartbeat.

❖ Gastrointestinal problems, such as heartburn, nausea, and diarrhea.

### TREATMENT

If you are bothered by anxiety, see your doctor, or another health professional. She or he may wish to prescribe special anti-anxiety medication for a short period of time only, since this type of drug tends to be addictive. Your doctor may also recommend counseling.

If you are taking other medications, be sure to let your doctor what they are, to avoid potentially harmful interactions. You should also abstain from alcohol for the same reason.

### WHAT YOU CAN DO

There are ways in which you can help yourself to cope with anxiety:

❖ Practise meditation and relaxation techniques daily.

❖ Stay fit.

❖ Try to identify your fears and confront them; you can overcome many fears once you understand the reasons underlying them.

❖ Learn and apply effective stress management techniques *(see page 70)*.

❖ If you can, postpone an event until you are confident that you can handle it.

❖ Be decisive: don't be afraid to make a decision and stick to it.

❖ Concentrate on today: yesterday is past and tomorrow may well depend on how you manage today (remind yourself that today is a gift, and that is why it is called "the present").

## DEPRESSIVE MOOD DISORDER

Mood has been described as a prolonged emotion that colors the psychic (mental) life. It has also been said to be a sustained and pervasive emotion that can have great influence on our perception of the world.

At some time in our life we all experience high and low points. Sad times are as much a part of life as happy times; sometimes we feel good about ourselves and sometimes we don't. Depressed persons, however, seem to experience a low mood for an extended period of time. When such a mood interferes substantially with day-to-day living, it is considered a "clinical depression" and requires treatment.

### SIGNS AND SYMPTOMS

Depression can change the way a person thinks and behaves. It can also affect the body's functions. Signs and symptoms that indicate a major depression include:

❖ Feeling joyless, helpless, hopeless, and worthless.

❖ Sleeping more or less than usual; early morning wakening.
❖ Marked anxiety.
❖ Having difficulty concentrating or making decisions.
❖ Loss of interest in usual activities; lack of motivation.
❖ Decreased interest in sex.
❖ Eating disturbances; changes in weight.
❖ Loss of energy; feeling fatigued.
❖ Thoughts of death or suicide.

Anyone who experiences four or more of these symptoms for more than two weeks should seek help.

**LEFT** *Putting on a brave face is not the way to overcome clinical depression.*

### CAUSES OF DEPRESSION

Despite everything that is known about depression, it is still not fully understood. Things that may precipitate or contribute to the illness include a distressing life event, a biochemical imbalance in the brain, inherited genes, or some medications used for other illnesses.

### TREATMENT

Depression is the most common form of psychiatric illness. It is also the most treatable. Most sufferers respond well to treatment that includes psychological counseling, support from a self-help group or from family and friends,

LEFT *If those around you are happy and yet you are unable to shift your long-running low mood, it is time to seek professional help.*

cognitive therapy, medications, electroconvulsive therapy (ECT, erroneously referred to as "shock treatment"), or a combination of these therapies.

## COGNITIVE THERAPY

The basis of cognitive therapy is the belief that the content and style of our thinking creates our overall mood. This means that distorted thoughts and self-defeating beliefs usually go on to generate painful feelings. These may take the form of low self-esteem, anxiety, depression, and anger.

Cognitive therapists work with clients, either in a one-to-one interaction or in a group setting, to help them to identify and change negative thought patterns in order to eventually alter the way they feel about themselves.

## MEDICATIONS

The full effects of antidepressant medications may not occur for about three or four weeks after starting treatment. Therefore, do not be disheartened if you do not see immediate or quick results. You will, however, often notice an improvement in sleep and appetite early in treatment.

Many people who have been taking antidepressant medications for some time discontinue them once they start to feel better. This is a great mistake. Antidepressants should be discontinued gradually, according to the doctor's prescription. Dosage is slowly reduced over a period of time.

## ECT

An electrical stimulus is delivered to the brain through electrodes applied to the temples. A seizure is produced by passing a current of 70–130 volts for 0.1–0.5 seconds through the electrodes. It is still not known exactly how ECT works toward alleviating depression and so the treatment remains controversial.

LEFT *One-to-one counseling can set a depressed person on the road to recovery.*

## POSTPARTUM DEPRESSION

Hormonal shifts immediately after childbirth can make women vulnerable to postpartum depression. This type of depression is not the same as the "blues" that often occur a few days after delivery. Rather, it is a frightening illness that appears between two weeks and 12 months after the baby's birth.

BELOW *Postpartum depression is a real illness, and it doesn't mean you don't love your baby.*

## SYMPTOMS

Any woman can experience postpartum depression, but those with a history of depression are more likely to do so than those who have never suffered from any form of depressive illness.

In its most severe form you may experience confusion, delusions, and sometimes hallucinations. You may even be so ill as to entertain thoughts of harming your baby. Less severe forms of this type of depression can appear about a month after delivery, but may last for months.

Aggravating or precipitating factors include: marital discord, conflicting feelings about being a mother, financial difficulties, and lack of family support.

## TREATMENT

Postpartum depression with psychotic features (such as hallucinations) should be treated immediately with appropriate medications (such as antidepressants and antipsychotic agents). Sometimes ECT is necessary. Please consult your doctor for treatment.

For forms of the depression not accompanied by psychosis, antidepressants, along with other therapies (such as "talk" therapy and cognitive therapy), have been found to be effective.

Women who have experienced postpartum depression should be cautious of taking oral contraceptives as they may contribute to further depression.

ABOVE *The Pill might not be the best choice contraception if you have suffered from postpartum depression.*

# BIPOLAR ILLNESS

Mood disorders generally fall into two types: depressive *(see pages 76–78)* and bipolar. An estimated one-third to one-half of all persons suffering from clinical depression are believed to have a bipolar illness (this was formerly known as manic depression).

## SYMPTOMS

The predominant symptom, which lasts from a few weeks to several months, is an elevated and expansive mood. Sudden shifts to irritability and anger and mood lability (cycles of highs and lows) are also characteristic. Other symptoms include:

❖ Increased activity and/ or restlessness.
❖ Feelings of grandeur.
❖ Racing thoughts.
❖ Talking a great deal, usually rapidly; this may sometimes take the form of incoherent speech.
❖ Increased sexual activity.
❖ Inappropriate social behavior.
❖ Decreased need for sleep and rest of any type.
❖ Very short attention span.
❖ Indecisiveness and making poor judgments.

As with depression, biochemical factors are thought to play a large role. Those who come from families with a history of the illness are considered more vulnerable to it than those who do not.

If you are in a manic state you may do things that are out of character and so create difficulties for those close to you. This may involve freely spending a great deal of money and getting into debt; or showing disregard for the law. You may also eat inadequately, lose weight, become sleep-deprived, and suffer poor health as a consequence.

## TREATMENT

Bipolar illness responds better to treatment than some other mental illnesses. With close medical supervision and appropriate supports (from family, for example), persons suffering from this disorder can usually be treated at home.

Treatment usually consists of medication (usually mood stabilizers such as lithium), psychological therapies, or a combination of both.

If you are taking lithium for bipolar illness, you should report regularly to your doctor or mental health center for routine blood tests, and you should also maintain an adequate fluid and sodium (salt) intake.

**ABOVE** *Bipolar illness can be treated with drugs, but a strong support network is also important.*

**BELOW** *Those suffering from the illness often eat badly; snacking on candies rather than eating a proper meal.*

## HELPFUL HINTS

⊙ Mood disorders are emotionally draining: they sap energy and self-esteem. They make the sufferer feel tired, worthless, helpless, and sometimes without hope. Seeking help from a doctor or other mental health professional is crucial.
⊙ Encouragement and strong support from family and close friends are vital to help sufferers recover.

## ANOREXIA NERVOSA

Commonly known as "anorexia," this eating disorder is characterized by an all-consuming preoccupation with food and dieting. Those afflicted with the illness feel fat, even when they are emaciated. Anorexia nervosa is 10–20 times more frequent in women than in men. The disorder usually appears in adolescence, and the incidence is greatest in high socio-economic groups *(see myths, on page 75)*, in high-achieving women, and in professions such as modeling and ballet, in which thinness is especially valued.

Anorexia nervosa appears to be a response to demands placed on adolescents, as they strive for more independence and also for increased social and sexual functioning. Those suffering from the illness (that often borders on obsession), substitute their preoccupation with eating and weight for other normal adolescent pursuits. They see themselves as much fatter than they are. However, it is not just an adolescent disorder: older females are also at risk of developing it.

ABOVE AND LEFT *Images of pencil-thin supermodels can be too much for some women, who take dieting to extremes.*

### DIAGNOSIS

For the diagnosis of anorexia nervosa to be made, there must be no known physical cause to account for the weight loss, and the failure to maintain expected weight must be marked: less than 85 percent of what would be considered normal body weight for the individual.

Anorexics have an intense fear of weight gain, distorted body image, and an extreme concern with body weight. Women usually experience amenorrhea (absent menstrual periods). Anorexia nervosa is one of the few psychiatric illnesses that may take a course leading to death. In any case, a woman who has been anorexic for a number of years is at risk of a number of medical conditions, which includes irregular heartbeat and osteoporosis.

## CHARACTERISTICS

❖ an irrational fear of body fat
❖ a desire to become thinner
❖ a misperception of body weight and shape to the extent that the person may feel "fat" even when emaciation is clear to others. These psychological characteristics contribute to drastic weight loss and defiant refusal to maintain a healthy weight for height and age.

## TREATMENT

The immediate aim of treatment is to restore the person's nutritional status to normal, since complications such as dehydration, emaciation, and disturbed body chemistry (electrolyte imbalance) may lead to death.

Treatment is consistent and structured, involving both behavior modification and nutritional counseling. Both the patient and their family are usually involved. Where necessary, appropriate medications (such as antidepressant agents) are prescribed. The final goal of treatment is the prevention of relapse.

BELOW AND RIGHT *Overcoming an eating disorder means restoring a healthy relationship with food.*

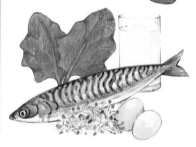

# BULIMIA NERVOSA

**ABOVE** *Obsessive self-criticism centered on weight and body shape is a symptom of bulimia nervosa.*

Usually referred to simply as "bulimia," this eating disorder occurs in five to 10 percent of young women.

Individuals with bulimia nervosa are typically ashamed of their eating problem and try to hide their symptoms. The binge-eating therefore occurs in secrecy, or as inconspicuously as possible, and also rapidly. This behavior is usually precipitated by low mood states, interpersonal stressors, intense hunger, or feelings related to body image. Although the binge-eating temporarily makes the person feel better, the self-criticism that follows generates a depressed mood and a lack of control.

Emphasis is put on body weight and shape and so a woman suffering from this condition may resemble an anorexia nervosa sufferer. However, individuals suffering from bulimia are usually within the normal weight range for their height.

## DIAGNOSIS

For a diagnosis of bulimia nervosa to be made, the following symptoms need to be present:

❖ Recurrent episodes of binge-eating about twice a week for three months.

❖ Recurrent inappropriate compensatory behavior, in order to prevent weight gain, such as self-induced vomiting, misuse of laxatives, diuretics, or enemas, fasting or excessive exercise.

❖ Extreme preoccupation with body weight and shape.

**ABOVE** *Bulimic women eat high fat food because of an outside problem they cannot control. They eat for comfort.*

## TREATMENT

Psychotherapy in the form of cognitive therapy *(see page 77)* is frequently employed. It is usually done on an individual basis. Medication, such as antidepressants, is also often used.

Goals of treatment are that the binge-eating and inappropriate compensatory behaviors cease, and that self-esteem should be built on factors more important than body weight and shape.

**BELOW** *Visiting a therapist is the best way to start solving an eating disorder. It is often best to invite supportive family or friends to go with you when you first attend.*

# 9 MONTHLY CYCLES

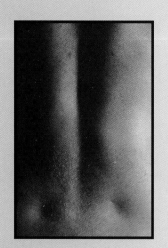

FROM A WOMAN'S INITIAL MENSTRUAL PERIOD (THE MENARCHE) TO THE TIME THAT MARKS PERMANENT CESSATION OF MENSTRUAL ACTIVITY (MENOPAUSE), SHE CAN EXPECT ABOUT 40 YEARS OF A MONTHLY CYCLE KNOWN AS MENSTRUATION. THE MENSTRUAL CYCLE PREPARES HER BODY FOR PREGNANCY. MENSTRUATION IS THE BODY'S WAY OF RIDDING ITSELF OF THE THICKENED INNER LINING OF THE WOMB WHERE NO PREGNANCY HAS TAKEN PLACE. THERE ARE MANY SYMPTOMS ASSOCIATED WITH MENSTRUATION, THE MOST PREVALENT OF WHICH IS PERIOD PAIN. IF PREGNANCY DOES NOT OCCUR, HER BODY ABANDONS ITS ELABORATE PREPARATIONS AND BEGINS A BRAND-NEW CYCLE.

## PHASES OF THE MENSTRUAL CYCLE

The menstrual cycle is usually thought of as lasting 28 days, but it can be as short as 18 or as long as 40 days.

**The proliferative phase** of the cycle (phase of rapid reproduction) lasts from 10 to 14 days. An ovum (egg) ripens in the ovary. The lining of the uterus (endometrium) becomes thicker and softer.

**The secretory phase** lasts from 10 to 14 days. In response to hormonal activity, the egg enters the corresponding fallopian tube. At this time, some women experience mid-cycle pain that is known as "mittelschmerz." Toward the end of this phase, the body tends to retain fluid, resulting in congestion and sometimes feelings of discomfort.

**The premenstrual phase** lasts one or two days. If the ovum is not fertilized, levels of hormones (estrogen and progesterone) drop sharply. Blood vessels within the uterus contract, supplying less nourishment to the endometrium, which consequently breaks down. Bleeding occurs and the uterine lining is shed. The abdominal cramps that many women experience shortly before menstrual bleeding starts are probably due to the degeneration of this lining.

**The menstrual phase** lasts for four or five days. Between 4 tbsp (60 ml) and 12 tbsp (180 ml) of fluid, containing blood cells, fragments of uterine lining, and various secretions, are discharged through the vagina. As this phase starts, other ova (eggs) start maturing to begin again with a whole new menstrual cycle.

**ABOVE** *There is no such thing as a "normal" menstrual cycle. Every woman is different.*

## PERIOD PAIN

Pain is usually the chief symptom reported by women experiencing menstrual difficulties.

Other symptoms include: backache, nausea, vomiting, headache, dizziness, nervousness, poor concentration, loss of appetite, and diarrhea. The range and severity of symptoms can vary greatly from woman to woman, and from month to month in the same woman.

## CAUSES

Chemical substances called PGs (prostaglandins), which are found in menstrual secretions, are suspected of causing some of the period pain (dysmenorrhea) women suffer from. PGs are hormone-like substances that play a role in the functioning of reproductive organs. They are present in many parts of the body, including the uterine lining. Their quantity increases significantly before menstruation,

and the menstrual secretions of women who ovulate contain about five times the amount of PGs of those of non-ovulating women (such as young women just starting their period or women who are using oral contraception). In fact, women who do not actually ovulate hardly ever complain of period pain.

PGs have a powerful effect on smooth muscle such as uterine muscle (myometrium). They cause the muscle to contract, and this appears to produce some of the pain of menstruation.

Other causes of period pain are actual disorders within the body itself: pelvic disease such as endometriosis (in which endometrium appears in areas other than the uterus, such as the pelvis or abdominal wall), fibroids (benign muscle tumors), IUD, ovarian cysts, and PID. These disorders are most common in women over the age of 30.

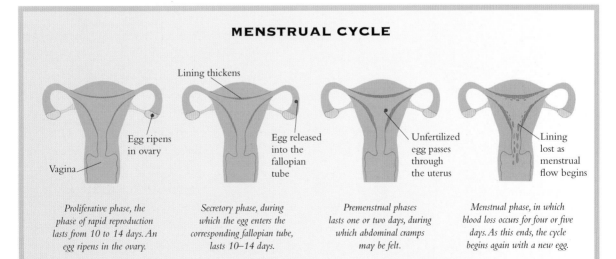

## MENSTRUAL CYCLE

Lining thickens

Egg ripens in ovary

Vagina

Egg released into the fallopian tube

Unfertilized egg passes through the uterus

Lining lost as menstrual flow begins

*Proliferative phase, the phase of rapid reproduction lasts from 10 to 14 days. An egg ripens in the ovary.*

*Secretory phase, during which the egg enters the corresponding fallopian tube, lasts 10–14 days.*

*Premenstrual phases lasts one or two days, during which abdominal cramps may be felt.*

*Menstrual phase, in which blood loss occurs for four or five days. As this ends, the cycle begins again with a new egg.*

## PREMENSTRUAL SYNDROME

PMS affects more than 90 percent of women at some point in their lives. PMS is defined as the occurrence of bothersome symptoms that develop, or worsen, during the two weeks before menstruation is expected. The symptoms disappear or ease dramatically in the 48 hours (sometimes within one or two hours) after the menstrual flow has begun. This is what distinguishes PMS from dysmenorrhea.

**BELOW** *PMS can affect a woman's mood, causing feelings of depression as well as lethargy. It may also be difficult to concentrate.*

### SYMPTOMS

These may be divided into physical and psychological categories:

❖ Physical symptoms include weight gain, painful breasts, water retention, swelling, headache, proneness to accidents, skin disorders, abnormal cravings, and various aches and pains.

❖ Psychological symptoms include increased tension; mood changes such as irritability, feelings of aggression and depression; lethargy, and reduced powers of concentration.

### CAUSES

The widespread belief that a deficiency of the hormone progesterone was the cause of PMS has recently fallen into disrepute. So has the theory that high estrogen levels are to blame. Some believe that another hormone called prolactin, the most important function of which is to stimulate the breasts to produce milk for the newborn baby, is a cause of the syndrome.

Although hormone balances do play a major role in the various manifestations of PMS, it is now believed that a lack of essential fatty acids (EFAs) is the probable common factor in the causation of premenstrual illness.

EFAs are essential for maintaining a healthy body and yet it cannot produce them itself, so they have to be provided by your diet. The best sources of EFAs are

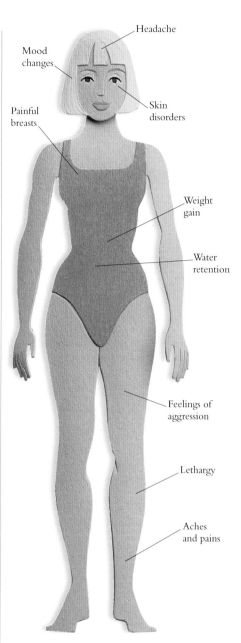

**ABOVE** *Some or all of the symptoms shown above are problems that are typical of PMS.*

Headache

Mood changes

Painful breasts

Skin disorders

Weight gain

Water retention

Feelings of aggression

Lethargy

Aches and pains

generally the oils of flax, safflower, sesame, sunflower, and evening primrose. Other good sources include corn, peanut and soybean oils, also almonds, avocados, green leafy vegetables, peanuts, pecan nuts, sunflower seeds, walnuts, and whole grains.

# PAIN RELIEF THROUGH MEDICATION

Various medications are used for relieving pain experienced during menstruation.

**Oral contraceptives (OCs):** most are a combination of estrogen and progestin. Their efficiency lies in their ability to suppress ovulation in about 80 percent of women. With the inhibition of ovulation, prostaglandin (PG) production is suppressed, thus lessening the uterine muscle contractions that lead to pain. However, it is worth considering whether hormone therapy that lasts for almost a whole month is justified in treating pain or discomfort that lasts only two or three days.

ABOVE *Don't let PMS affect the rest of your life. Investigate the options for relieving the symptoms.*

BELOW *Abdominal cramps might not last long, but they can be painful and depressing.*

**Estrogens:** these can be used alone to convert an ovulatory cycle into an anovulatory (not preceded by ovulation) one so as to bring pain relief with the next menstrual flow. Regrettably, relatively high doses are required to produce this effect, and this may in turn cause unfortunate side effects such as nausea and excessive bleeding.

**Progestogens:** synthetic progestogens, which have progesterone-like activity, are less effective than estrogens in the management of menstrual pain. The use of powerful hormones for 21 days a month to control one or two days of period pain is not recommended for women who do not need contraception for any other reason.

**PG inhibitors:** also called PGSIs (protaglandin synthetase inhibitors or non-steroidal anti-inflammatory drugs – NSAIDs). These powerful drugs are designed to interrupt or inhibit the action of PGs, to bring about a corresponding reduction of pressure within the uterus. Blood loss is also decreased, and so contributes to pain relief.

There are many kinds of PG inhibitors on the market and they are all generally similar and of varying efficacy in alleviating the symptoms of period pain. They include aspirin, indocin, mefenamic acid, naproxen, and ibuprofen.

**Antidepressants:** these are drugs with properties that relieve the symptoms of depression that may occur during premenstrual syndrome *(see page 76).*

## NATURAL PAIN CONTROL

Many doctors or other therapists rely exclusively on medications to provide pain relief to women experiencing dysmenorrhea. However, consideration should also be given to the mind-body interdependence, and to the perception of pain that is influenced by psychological factors such as attitude, anxiety, attention, suggestion, and personal variables.

Everyone has the potential to limit, control, or even prevent pain through mind power. Natural pain control methods (such as those used in childbirth) are largely based on the "spinal gate control" theory. Simply explained, there appears to be a nervous mechanism which, in effect, opens or closes a "gate" that controls pain stimuli traveling to the brain for interpretation. This mechanism can be influenced by certain psychological factors, like those mentioned above.

Natural pain control methods, such as certain yoga techniques, are largely based on closing the spinal "gate" so that pain stimuli do not reach the brain. They are safer than pain management practices that depend only on drugs. They work by mobilizing the body's own resources to promote comfort and a sense of well-being, and they are free of unwanted side effects.

### BREATHING EXERCISES

A close relationship exists between our respiratory (breathing) system and our perception of, and response to, pain. Breathing accelerates and becomes shallow when we experience pain or discomfort, and it may even be irregular or difficult.

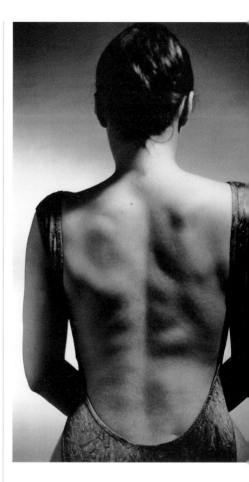

RIGHT *It is possible to learn natural methods of pain control that are free from the unwanted side-effects associated with some drugs.*

When we are at ease, however, breathing is usually slow and regular. Practicing voluntary controlled breathing is one way to decrease the perception of pain, and the anxiety, tension, and fear that often accompany or aggravate it.

Suggested breathing exercises to help you cope with pain include alternate nostril breathing, the anti-anxiety breath, the cleansing breath, and the divided breath on pages 44–48. Other techniques useful in helping to increase your tolerance of pain and discomfort may be found in mindwork, pages 50–59.

LEFT *Breathing techniques to help women cope with labor can also be used to relieve other forms of pain.*

## PHYSICAL EXERCISE

Studies have shown that women who exercise regularly tend to cope better with pain than those who do not. Regular exercise makes available greater amounts of endorphins (morphine-like substances occurring naturally in the brain), which act as a natural pain-reliever.

Particularly useful for period pain sufferers is the stretching, slow-moving type of exercise done in synchronization with regular breathing *(see the mini-workout on page 36)*. If you practice such exercises faithfully when not menstruating, you should see an improvement in distressing menstrual symptoms in about three months. Other good exercises are the warm-up for legs (the butterfly exercise) and the rock-and-roll for the whole body *(see page 35)*.

In addition, try to engage in some form of aerobic exercise, such as brisk walking, cycling, and swimming, for half an hour or more three times a week to stimulate your heart and lungs, before your menstrual period starts.

**RIGHT AND FAR RIGHT** *Regular exercise releases endorphins, the body's natural pain-relievers.*

## DIET AND LIFESTYLE CHANGES FOR PAIN RELIEF

Food is both a source of comfort and sustenance, appeasing hunger and providing essential nutrients for health and well-being. Most foods can fulfill the former requirement, but only those that are "whole" will contribute significantly to the latter.

Whole foods are those that have not had anything added to them or taken away through processing. They are unrefined foods, in their natural state, free of chemical additives, and, most importantly, have high nutrient value. They include fresh fruits and vegetables (unsprayed and unwaxed), wholemeal flour, whole grains and cereals, pulses, and nuts.

By changing your diet you can alleviate some of the symptoms associated with period pain and PMS, and there are other measures you can take to ease discomforts, including stress management and therapeutic baths.

### DIET

Among the nutrients that seem to affect symptoms are sodium (salt), vitamin B6 (pyridoxine), and magnesium.

Too much sodium in the diet may contribute to swelling of the tissues because of water retention, and a consequent feeling of bloatedness. Swelling is not always

**ABOVE** *Take small but positive steps to improve your diet and you are more likely to succeed than if you make sweeping changes.*

confined to the hands and feet, but may also spread to eye tissue. Doctors often prescribe diuretics ("water pills") for this problem. But in helping to rid the body of surplus fluid, these agents unfortunately also increase the loss, through the urine, of important substances such as potassium.

To help minimize discomforts related to fluid retention, it is best to decrease your salt intake and to increase your consumption of foods that are naturally diuretic such as asparagus, cranberry juice, kelp (seaweed), peaches, watercress, and watermelon, as well as foods rich in vitamin B6 and magnesium *(see pages 22–29),* rather than depend on artificial means that can cause other problems.

**RIGHT** *Even small changes in your diet, like drinking cranberry juice, can bring about huge improvements in your health and well-being.*

## SOOTHING TISANE

⊙ Mix together 1 oz (28 g) each of camomile, cowslip, linden, and violet flowers.

⊙ Store the resulting herbal blend in an airtight container in a cool, dark place – it is now ready for use whenever you want to. You now have the raw ingredients to make numerous delicious and soothing drinks.

⊙ When needed, pour 18 fl oz (500 ml) boiling water over 2 tbsp (30 ml) of the mixed herbs.

⊙ Let it steep for about 20 minutes before straining and drinking.

⊙ Note that linden is a mild sedative and violet flowers contain salicylic acid (a pain-reliever) and vitamins A and C.

## HERBAL TEAS

There is now a huge choice of herbal teas available on the market. These are all good alternatives to caffeinated drinks. They also have relaxing and diuretic properties.

It can be extremely rewarding to make, or even create, your own teas. Herbal teas are generally known as "tisanes." Below and right are two recipes for particularly soothing tisanes.

## DIURETIC TISANE

Mix together 1 oz (28 g) each of alfalfa, camomile flowers, comfrey leaves, dandelion leaves, elderflowers, and lemon peel. Store the resulting blend of herbs in an airtight container in a cool and dark place.

When needed, pour 18 fl oz (500 ml) boiling water over 2 tbsp (30 ml) of the mixed herbs. Let the mixture steep for about 20 minutes before straining and drinking.

## EMOTIONAL STATE

The menstrual cycle is very sensitive to changes in emotional states. In London during World War II, gynecologists observed an amazing number of cases of amenorrhea (absent menstrual periods). As the women lost their anxieties, their periods returned. Similarly, women who travel a great deal or experience major lifestyle changes tend to miss their periods for a certain amount of time.

Learning and practicing effective stress management strategies *(see page 70)* will help to lessen the unpleasant symptoms often associated with menstruation.

**BELOW** *The menstrual cycle is affected by changes in lifestyle, particularly when events beyond our control cause stress.*

## COMFORT MEASURES

Baths have been used for centuries to promote sleep, allay muscle spasms, relieve aching joints and muscles, soothe itching, and improve blood circulation. They can be a great help in soothing menstruation pain.

**Epsom salts bath**: dissolve 1 lb (454 g) Epsom salts (magnesium sulfate – available at pharmacies) in a bathtub of warm water. Soak in it for 15 minutes to relax your muscles and relieve joint stiffness.

**Herbal bath**: put a handful of mixed herbs of your choice in a small drawstring bag (for example, basil, camomile flowers, lavender, marigold petals, peppermint, red clover, rosemary, sage, or spearmint). Close the bag and hang it on the faucet so that it is immersed in the water as the bathtub fills. As you soak in the tub for 15 minutes, you will be able to savor a feeling of luxury imparted by the aromatic oils released from the herbs.

**Sitz bath**: this is excellent for relieving pain and congestion. Fill a hip bath or large, deep bowl with enough water so that when you sit in it your pelvis is submerged. The water temperature should be maintained between 100° and 115°F (38° and 46°C). Your feet should not be in the water. Remain in the bath for 10–20 minutes, and keep your upper body warm.

**ABOVE** *Make your own aromatherapy bath with bundles of fragrant herbs.*

## MENOPAUSE

The period that marks the permanent cessation of menstrual activity is known as menopause. It usually occurs between 35 and 58 years of age, the average being 51 years. The menstrual periods may stop suddenly; there may be a decreased flow each month; or the interval between periods may lengthen until final cessation.

BELOW *Being aware of the changes that take place during the menopause will leave you better equipped to cope with them.*

## SYMPTOMS

As women approach menopause, many physiological changes related to a decrease in estrogen take place in their bodies. The symptoms generally associated with menopause begin shortly after ovarian function ceases. This is true regardless of whether menopause occurs naturally or as a result of the surgical removal of the ovaries.

### CHECKLIST

Symptoms may last from a few months to years, and vary from being hardly noticeable to very severe. They include:

- ⊙ Nervousness.
- ⊙ Hot flushes.
- ⊙ Chills.
- ⊙ Apathy.
- ⊙ Excitability.
- ⊙ Fatigue.
- ⊙ Mental depression.
- ⊙ Unstable mood.
- ⊙ Insomnia.
- ⊙ Heart palpitations.
- ⊙ Vertigo.
- ⊙ Headache.
- ⊙ Numbness.
- ⊙ Tingling.
- ⊙ Muscle pain.
- ⊙ Urinary disturbances.
- ⊙ Various disorders of the stomach and intestines.

## HORMONE REPLACEMENT THERAPY

Many doctors recommend hormone replacement therapy (HRT) for the relief of menopausal symptoms. Before accepting this therapy, you need to be informed so you can weigh up the potential benefits against possible risks. The benefits are good. There is a decreased risk of cardiovascular disease and the prevention or lessening of osteoporosis (increased porosity of bones) when using HRT. With a low estrogen dosage, the risk of breast cancer is not increased. By adding progesterone, the risk of endometrial cancer is virtually eliminated.

Not every woman, however, is a good candidate for HRT, and there are contraindications because some women experience side effects such as withdrawal bleeding (cyclical bleeding) and with it a fear of pregnancy, periodic breast tenderness, a return of premenstrual tension, and sometimes weight gain. Some women also report an increase in libido. You need to evaluate your own situation very carefully and find out about the normal changes due to decreased estrogen production; talk to your doctor, and know your own personal health status before deciding whether to accept or reject HRT.

LEFT *Taking HRT is a big decision so make sure you are fully informed about all the options.*

# NATURAL ALTERNATIVES

There are many reliable natural alternatives to synthetic hormones that will alleviate menopausal symptoms without the risks associated with traditional hormone therapy.

**ALFALFA SPROUTS**

**ALFALFA** The leaves of the alfalfa plant are an excellent diuretic. However, alfalfa can aggravate lupus *(see page 118)*.

**DANDELION**
An excellent diuretic, dandelion is also rich in potassium, a mineral that is excreted when synthetic diuretics are used. The leaves can be used to make a tea, or can be added to salads.

**DONG QUAI** Highly prized in Asia, dong quai is known as female ginseng. It has mild estrogen properties, and so can help to relieve hot flushes and other unpleasant menopausal symptoms. However, it can cause some people to suffer from insomnia.

**GINSENG** Rich in a plant form of estrogen, ginseng has been used successfully to relieve hot flushes. American or Siberian ginseng can be preferable to the Asian type, which some people find too stimulating. Do not use ginseng if you suffer from high blood pressure or have any irregular heartbeats. Let your doctor know if you are using ginseng, particularly if you experience any irregular bleeding during menopause.

GINSENG

**GINSENG ROOT**

**HOPS** This herb, which is rich in plant estrogens, has soothing and relaxing properties. It is especially useful in helping to combat insomnia.

Dong quai and ginseng help alleviate hot flushes

Hops help you relax and sleep

Alfalfa and dandelion are good diuretics

**ABOVE** *There are natural alternatives to drug treatments for many symptoms of the menopause.*

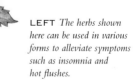

**HOPS**

**LEFT** *The herbs shown here can be used in various forms to alleviate symptoms such as insomnia and hot flushes.*

**DANDELION**

## DIET FOR THE MENOPAUSE

Hot flushes are rare in Japan, so much so that there is no word or phrase for the symptom. Japanese women eat plenty of soybean products such as tofu and tempeh and drink soy milk, all excellent sources of plant compounds that behave like estrogen in the body (they are called phytoestrogens).

**BELOW** *Alfalfa, sprouts, potatoes, rice, rye, barley, wheat, yams, apples, and cherries are all good sources of phytoestrogens.*

Other foods that are rich in these compounds include alfalfa, apples, barley, cherries, potatoes, rice, rye, wheat, yams, and yeast.

Eating for energy, pages 20–31, shows you the essential nutrients needed to promote and maintain health at any age. It also shows you the food sources of the nutrients.

## STRESS AND THE MENOPAUSE

It is essential to well-being at any age to have the ability to cope with day-to-day events and with inevitable crisis. This is particularly true at the time of the menopause and later life. Developing and practicing the art of stress management from an early age is one of the best "tools" at your disposal for a healthy, prosperous life.

**ABOVE** *Japanese women do not experience the hot flushes that Western women do because their diet is rich in soy products, which contain phytoestrogens.*

There are techniques and suggestions that are extremely beneficial for the menopause in this book. These include breathwork *(see page 40)*, mindwork *(see page 50)*, and stress management *(see page 70)*.

Remember that menopause is not a disease. Although it may generate a number of stresses, it may also herald rewarding times and the potential for personal development. In addition to any medical interventions that may be necessary, you can also draw upon your own natural resources: body, mind, and breath.

# 10 PREGNANCY AND AFTER

THE PREPARATION FOR CHILDBIRTH SHOULD START WELL BEFORE A WOMAN CONCEIVES, FOR THE HEALTHIER THE BODY IN WHICH A CHILD BEGINS LIFE, THE BETTER THE CHANCES OF A SUCCESSFUL OUTCOME OF ANY PREGNANCY. THINK ALSO OF THE CHILDBEARING YEARS AS INCLUDING NOT ONLY THE ROUGHLY NINE MONTHS OF ANY PREGNANCY, BUT ALSO THE CRITICAL POSTPARTUM PERIOD (THE TIME IMMEDIATELY FOLLOWING DELIVERY). IN THE EXCITEMENT SURROUNDING LABOR AND THE BIRTH ITSELF, IT IS EASY TO FORGET THE CAREFUL PHYSICAL AND MENTAL CONDITIONING REQUIRED FOR A RAPID RETURN OF STAMINA AND EFFICIENCY, AND THE PREVENTION OF COMPLICATIONS.

## COMMON DISCOMFORTS

During pregnancy, a woman may experience one or more of a number of minor discomforts. Although these may not in themselves be serious, they tend to detract from a feeling of complete well-being. They include nausea and vomiting, motion sickness and dizziness, indigestion and heartburn, flatulence and constipation, various symptoms due to pressure – such as swelling of hands and feet – varicose veins, hemorrhoids, leg cramps, shortness of breath, backache, insomnia, and mood changes.

ABOVE *The joy of pregnancy can be somewhat dampened by discomfort but there are plenty of things that can be done to alleviate it.*

## NAUSEA AND VOMITING

Hormonal changes and emotional adjustments, particularly in the first three or four months of pregnancy, are the usual causes of nausea and vomiting. To lessen the occurrence and severity of these symptoms, which seem worse when the stomach is empty, have frequent snacks of fresh fruit, plain whole-wheat crackers or other nutritious lowfat items. Keep meals smaller, plainer, and lighter than usual, and sip red raspberry leaf or spearmint tea.

Check with your doctor or other caregiver about the safe use of herbs in pregnancy: pregnant women should not use any herbs for medicinal purposes without the approval of their doctor but these may help alleviate symptoms. Also practice slow, deep breathing (*see page 40*).

## MOTION SICKNESS AND DIZZINESS

A sudden change from a lying or semi-reclining position to an upright one can precipitate these symptoms. Always remember to get up slowly and with awareness.

Motion sickness can also be a result of lowered blood sugar level. Eating nutritious snacks every couple of hours or so could counteract this. Also practice slow, deep breathing for relief.

**ABOVE** *Sips of water, dry crackers, or other foods to raise the blood sugar can help counteract feelings of nausea.*

## INDIGESTION AND HEARTBURN

Following the suggestions in the section on nausea and vomiting will help to ease these two symptoms. Eating foods rich in the B vitamins also helps to prevent or counteract indigestion and heartburn (*see page 23*).

Check with your doctor or other caregiver before using antacids. Do not use bicarbonate of soda to relieve heartburn, since its sodium (salt) content is much too high.

**LEFT** *Eating foods rich in Vitamin B should help to alleviate or even prevent severe heartburn.*

## FLATULENCE

Flatulence in pregnancy is usually a result of bacterial action, which produces excessive gas, and also reduces stomach acid and affects the normal balance of hormones.

Measures for relief are the same as for nausea (*see above*), and also taking care to prevent constipation (*see below*). In addition, practice squatting regularly, every day, unless you have varicose veins.

## CONSTIPATION

Avoid using commercial laxatives, particularly mineral oil, which can deplete your body of essential nutrients. Make sure your intake of water, dietary fiber, and the B vitamins is adequate.

Practice the Complete Breath (*see page 46*) several times every day, and maintain a regular exercising program approved by your doctor or other caregiver.

## PRESSURE SYMPTOMS

As pregnancy progresses, the enlarging uterus places pressure on pelvic blood vessels. This interferes, to some extent, with the return blood flow to the heart, and generally slows down the circulation. Poor posture and lax abdominal muscles aggravate the situation, causing symptoms such as:

**BELOW** *The pressure of an enlarging uterus due to the rapid growth of the baby can cause problems with circulation. This can be made even worse by bad posture.*

❖ Swelling of hands and feet. Body fluids tend to collect in limbs that hang downward, causing swelling (edema). When these parts are elevated, the fluid is given a chance to redistribute itself. Therefore, sit with your legs raised whenever you can, and try not to cross them. Frequent changes of position also help to maintain good circulation. Since salt encourages fluid retention, some doctors encourage pregnant clients to restrict their salt intake. Follow your own doctor's instructions.

❖ Varicose veins. Try to walk every day and pay attention to good posture. Practice the Complete Breath exercise regularly (*see page 46*), as it also contributes to good circulation. Do not wear restrictive garments such as "knee-highs," garters, or tight bras. See also the previous point on swelling.

❖ Hemorrhoids. These are a form of varicose veins, which can protrude from the rectum. They may itch, cause pain, or even bleed. Any medication for their relief should be prescribed by a doctor. Avoid becoming constipated (*see previous page*).

❖ Leg cramps. Deficiency of iron, calcium, or the B vitamins can contribute to leg cramps, so ensure an adequate daily intake of these nutrients. For relief of sudden leg cramp, flex your ankle: pull the toes toward you and push the heel away from you. If you are lying down, it may help to stand up.

❖ Shortness of breath. This is usually more noticeable toward the end of pregnancy because of the pressure of the uterus against the diaphragm. Difficult breathing may be more evident when you are sitting than when you are standing.

Arrange pillows to give support to your head and shoulders. Periodically raise your arms above your head to expand your rib cage and improve your air intake. Pay attention to good posture.

If shortness of breath is coupled with marked fatigue, you may be deficient of iron or any the B vitamins. Discuss your symptoms with your doctor.

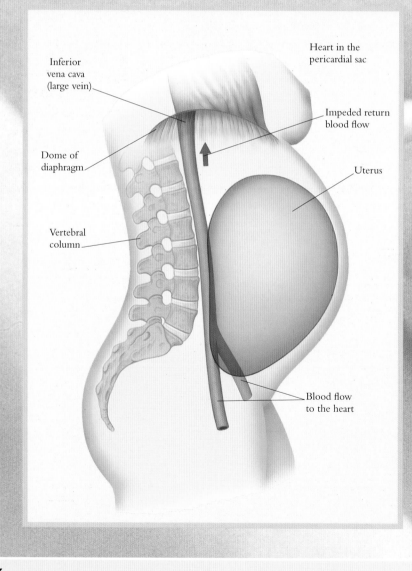

Heart in the pericardial sac

Inferior vena cava (large vein)

Impeded return blood flow

Dome of diaphragm

Uterus

Vertebral column

Blood flow to the heart

## BACKACHE

A hormone called relaxin literally relaxes certain joints and ligaments during pregnancy. This is one reason why some women suffer from backache.

To reduce the occurrence of backache, make sure your posture is good, regardless of whether you are sitting, standing, or walking, and regularly practice exercises approved by your doctor to strengthen your back and abdomen.

## INSOMNIA

Sleeplessness is a common problem in late pregnancy. Since the causes of insomnia are numerous, it is best to try to identify the specific factors underlying this difficulty, and to take steps to remedy them *(see sleep management on page 14 for suggestions on how to obtain sound, restful sleep).*

Do not use any sedatives or tranquilizers, or even herbal remedies, without first getting your doctor's permission.

## MOOD CHANGES

Because of the many changes taking place in a woman's body during pregnancy, it is not surprising that fluctuations in mood are common. In trying to pinpoint possible causes for mood swings, examine lifestyle factors such as nutrition, exercise, rest, relaxation, sleep, support networks, and interpersonal communication *(see also mental health, pages 74–81).*

**LEFT** *Reduce the tiring effects of nagging backache with good posture and gentle exercise.*

# HEALTHY PREGNANCY CHECKLIST

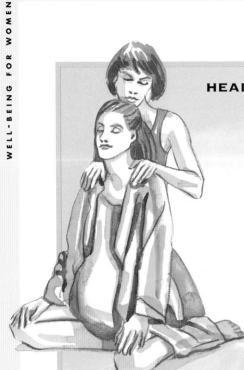

ABOVE *Your partner or a friend will be called upon to give you mental and physical support.*

⊙ Establish and maintain a reliable support system, which might consist of your partner, a trusted friend, a dependable relative, and/or other person with whom you have a good rapport.

⊙ Visit your doctor regularly.

BELOW *Gentle exercise, such as swimming, is good for pregnancy.*

Questions to ask your doctor might include:

**1** Is the baby's father allowed in the labor and delivery rooms?

**2** Do you have a choice of body position during delivery (alternatives to lying on your back with your feet in stirrups)?

**3** What-pain relief medications are available, should they be required? What are their possible side effects, if any?

**4** Under what circumstances does the doctor find it necessary to use intravenous fluids; artificially rupture membranes; or employ continuous fetal electronic monitoring?

**5** Is follow-up care available at home?

⊙ See your dentist before a planned pregnancy or early in your pregnancy. Maintain good dental hygiene and adhere to an adequate diet as pregnant women are particularly susceptible to gum problems and tooth decay.

⊙ Participate in antenatal classes and encourage your partner to do the same.

⊙ Be knowledgeable about pregnancy: physical and psychological changes that occur; sexual relations; growth and development of the fetus; exercise, nutrition, and stress management; smoking, drugs, and alcohol, etc. Many excellent books on pregnancy, birth, breastfeeding, and other related topics are available in bookstores and libraries. *See also bibliography, page 126.*

ABOVE *Write down questions you need to ask the health professionals to be sure you don't forget them.*

⊙ Exercise daily and maintain good posture. Include in your exercise program, breathing, some form of meditative exercise, and also tension-relieving and other relaxation techniques *(see pages 32–49)*. Check with your own doctor about the appropriateness of each of the exercises you wish to do.

## LABOR

Labor is a normal process that leads to the delivery of the baby and the placenta (afterbirth). It starts approximately 40 weeks after the first day of the last menstrual period. It consists of three stages: first, second, and third.

The first stage covers the onset of labor until the woman's cervix is fully dilated. The second stage is the delivery of the baby, and in the last stage the placenta is expelled.

Everything positive you do before and during pregnancy is, in effect, preparation for labor and delivery. Your two greatest allies in labor are your birth partner – the person who will be with you to give encouragement and support – and your breath. The breathing exercises you practice in pregnancy and the ones you learn in antenatal classes will serve you well.

### FIRST STAGE

Uterus

During this first stage of labor, the normally thick, tough cervix (neck of the womb) shortens and becomes thin (effecement). The opening of the cervix widens, or dilates, to about 4 in (10 cm), which is about the width of five fingers.

This initial stage is usually longer with a first baby than it is with subsequent births, and it can last as long as 32 hours, although it usually averages about 12 hours. Uterine contractions occur every 5–20 minutes in this stage, and each lasts for approximately 35–40 seconds.

### SECOND STAGE

Placenta

During this stage, the baby is pushed through the birth canal. This stage lasts about one hour. Contractions occur every 2–3 minutes and last 60–90 seconds.

### THIRD STAGE

Umbilical cord

During the final stage of labor, the uterus contracts to become smaller as the placenta is expelled in around 5–20 minutes.

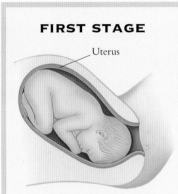

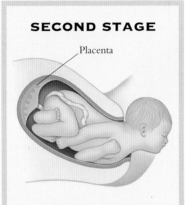

RIGHT *When a couple becomes a loving family, life changes more than you could possibly imagine.*

## CAESAREAN BIRTH

Caesarean birth, often referred to as Caesarean section or "C-sec" is when a baby is delivered through incisions in the walls of the abdomen and the uterus.

The purpose of a Caesarean section is to preserve the life or health of the mother and/or the baby. The most common reason for this procedure is when the baby's head is too large to pass through the birth canal. Other reasons include failure of labor to progress normally; certain changes in the rate and pattern of the baby's heartbeat; certain medical conditions of the mother (such as diabetes or high blood pressure); and the position of the baby, the umbilical cord, or the placenta.

*BELOW Make a birth plan, but be prepared to be flexible and to react appropriately as the labor progresses.*

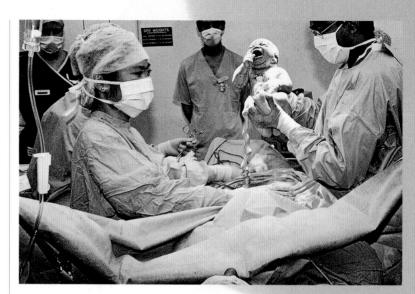

*ABOVE If you are going to have a Caesarean birth, try to find out as much as you can beforehand.*

### FEELINGS

It is normal for a pregnant woman to feel some apprehension about the outcome of her pregnancy. When facing the prospect of a Caesarean birth the anxiety can intensify. Knowing what to expect and how best to cope are two of your best defenses against uncertainty and fear.

Attend a class especially designed for women anticipating Caesarean birth, or attend a regular antenatal class and let your instructor know your circumstances. Encourage your partner to attend classes with you. Above all, be reassured that you are not a failure because you are going to deliver your baby by this method. One third of all women giving birth in developed countries will do so surgically, and there are numerous reasons for doing so.

### BEFORE SURGERY

If you know beforehand that you will be giving birth by Caesarean section, it is still beneficial to practice breathing and relaxation techniques. Also practice back and abdominal exercises, and maintain good posture.

During the actual Caesarean itself, it can help to arrange to have someone you love and trust with you (if this is permitted), since his or her presence can drastically reduce the accompanying apprehension.

## ANESTHESIA

Anesthesia may either be general, during which you are asleep, or epidural, during which you are awake. The latter is introduced by injection into the nerve pathways of the lower part of the spine, and produces a temporary loss of sensation below the lower ribs.

## AFTER SURGERY

Your stay in hospital after a Caesarean section may be two or three days longer than with a vaginal birth. Your baby may be kept in an incubator for a few hours for close observation, but will be brought to you for feeding.

**BELOW** *Even if your baby is in an incubator, hospital staff will give you every opportunity to bond with him or her.*

## OPTIONS

You may not have the final say in how your baby will be born. You do, however, have certain choices if you know in advance that you are going to have your baby by Caesarean section. Some of these options are:

❖ Requesting admission to hospital on the morning of surgery, rather than the day before – if you prefer.

❖ Requesting only partial pre-operative preparation, rather than the full routine which includes extensive shaving and an enema.

❖ Requesting information on medications you may be given.

❖ Being allowed to discuss a choice of anesthesia.

**ABOVE** *Don't be discouraged if breastfeeding seems rather a struggle at first. Both you and your baby need to learn how to do it.*

❖ Asking for permission for your partner or other helper to be present at the birth, if circumstances permit this.

❖ Asking to hold and nurse your baby as soon as possible after birth.

❖ Requesting minimal restrictions on visiting for the child's father.

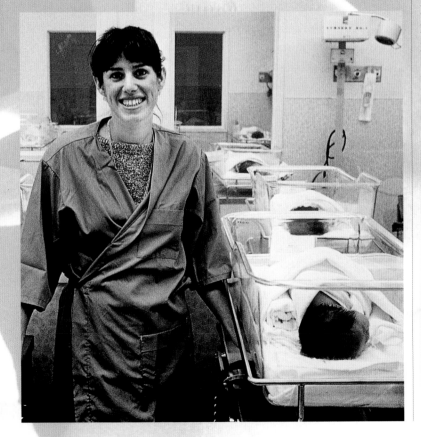

## HELPFUL HINTS

⊙ The fact that a woman has had her first birth by Caesarean section does not necessarily mean that she will automatically have subsequent births by the same route as each pregnancy is different.

⊙ Take advantage of any existing Caesarean support group that may be available in your community.

## THE POSTPARTUM PERIOD

The postpartum period is the time immediately following the birth of your baby. Directly after delivery, your temperature, pulse, and blood pressure will be monitored. During the days and months following, your body begins to change. This is when the reproductive organs begin their return toward the non-pregnant state. The most marked changes occur in the breasts, the abdomen, and the pelvic organs.

## THE BREASTS

During your pregnancy, your milk-producing glands will have started working, and your breasts will have enlarged. In appearance, the breasts do not alter noticeably in the first two or three days after the baby is born. During this time, they secrete "colostrum," a thin, yellowish fluid abundant in nutrients. Between the third and fourth days postpartum, milk starts to replace colostrum. The breasts then become engorged. The resulting discomfort usually disappears in a day or two.

## THE ABDOMEN

In the nine or so months of pregnancy, the abdominal wall has stretched immensely. When this tension from the enlarged uterus is relaxed, following childbirth, the abdomen becomes flabby. With proper care, however, the abdominal muscles should approach their original tone in two or three months. Check with your doctor or physiotherapist about suitable graduated exercises to do regularly to help you to regain abdominal muscle tone and strength.

## GRADUATED POSTPARTUM EXERCISES

The following are just a couple of examples of useful exercises. Begin them within 24 hours of delivery. Repeat each exercise twice to begin with, and then progress at your own pace. After each exercise, spend a minute or two relaxing and breathing deeply. Do the exercises at least twice daily.

### Abdominal Tightening

1 Lie on your back with your knees bent.
2 Take a deep inward breath through your nostrils.
3 Exhale through pursed lips (as described on page 45) while tightening your abdomen.
4 Relax your mouth. Inhale through your nostrils.
5 Repeat steps 3 and 4. Rest.

BELOW *Regular, gentle exercise will help you regain your figure surprisingly quickly.*

### Ankle Circling

1 Lie on your back, with your legs stretched out in front of you. Breathe slowly and smoothly through your nostrils.
2 Raise one leg. Slowly circle the ankle, first clockwise then counterclockwise, a few times in each direction.
3 Rest your leg and foot.
4 Repeat step 2 with the other ankle. Rest.

You may practice ankle circling while sitting: rotate the left ankle clockwise, then the right counter-clockwise a few times. Then repeat in the other direction.

Circle your ankle

Breathe through your nostrils

**ABOVE** *Plenty of fresh air is good for you and your baby. Don't forget to include older siblings as much as you can.*

## PELVIC ORGANS

Your doctor will probably wish to examine you about six weeks after your baby's birth. She or he will check to determine if your uterus has returned to normal and is not displaced, and that your perineum (the tissues between your anus and external genitals) has healed well. Now you may ask about gradually resuming the exercises you did antenatally. You will find the exercises on pages 32–39 useful: modify them to suit your level of flexibility and strength, and your feeling of comfort with them. You may also wish to take a look at books that will give you suitable exercises *(see bibliography, page 126).*

Add to your exercise program a period of daily walking to promote normal blood circulation, and also practice deep diaphragmatic breathing, such as the complete breath *(see page 46).* Daily relaxation is also crucial to a speedy return of stamina and efficiency, and to successful breastfeeding *(see pages 50–59).*

## "FIFTH DAY BLUES"

Some women become depressed about the fifth day after childbirth *(see the postpartum section on page 78).* Breathing techniques such as alternate nostril breathing and the anti-anxiety breath *(see pages 44–45),* and relaxation exercises like complete relaxation *(see page 56)* are useful in helping to cope with the resulting difficult emotions.

**BELOW** *When your baby is sleeping, take the chance to relax for a while. The housework can wait.*

# 11 FOR OLDER WOMEN

OLDER ADULTS REPRESENT THE FASTEST-GROWING SEGMENT OF MANY OF THE POPULATIONS IN COUNTRIES TODAY. THEY ARE LIVING LONGER THAN THEIR ANCESTORS DID, AND EXPERTS PREDICT THAT THIS TREND WILL CONTINUE. SOME OLDER WOMEN SEE THE YEARS AHEAD OF THEM IN TERMS OF LONELINESS AND DESPAIR BECAUSE OF A PERCEIVED LOSS OF ALL THOSE THINGS THAT GAVE THEM THEIR SENSE OF WORTH: EMPLOYMENT AND PARENTING, FOR EXAMPLE. IN ADDITION, THE PHYSICAL CHANGES THAT HERALD THE PERMANENT DEPARTURE OF YOUTH MAY ADD TO THESE FEELINGS OF WORTHLESSNESS, AND THE SCENE IS SET FOR A MAJOR DEPRESSION.

## LIVING FULLY AND JOYFULLY

The bleak scenario of losing employment due to retirement and children leaving the family home can cause depression for women who have nothing to replace these things. However, many older women refuse to allow society to make them feel unattractive, useless, and perhaps even a nuisance. Life's later decades should be regarded as a

**ABOVE** *With good health, you can go on enjoying life long after retiring from work.*

period in which to reflect with pride and pleasure on your contributions to family, the work force, and society at large.

Try viewing later life as the opportunity for well-earned freedom, for continued growth, and for much-deserved contentment. Then, living long will become not nearly as important as making sure you live fully and joyfully.

Life's later years can be exciting and rewarding, but only if you keep yourself fit enough to enjoy them. Few things are sadder than being "retired" and financially secure, yet not well enough to enjoy the fruits of your toil; to savor your meals; or have time for solitude without equating it with loneliness.

## PHYSICAL CHANGES

As women age, certain physical changes inevitably occur such as:

**Spine:** loss of height due to decreased bone mass and drying out of intervertebral discs, which cushion spinal bones.

**Postural:** gradual stooping, slight bending forward, and some flexing of the knees and hips as bone mass decreases and muscle tone wastes away.

**Weight:** some weight loss can be expected after the age of 60.

**Facial:** some loss of skin tone and addition of fine wrinkling; dryness of the skin; and a decrease in the size of the lower face due to bone loss in the jaw bone.

**Chest:** increased anterior-posterior (front to back) diameter of the chest to correspond with some loss of lung elasticity.

**Breathing:** increased rigidity of the rib cage due to bone changes causes decreased ventilation of lungs. Decreased strength of the diaphragm contributes to difficulty in breathing out.

**Nervous system:** reaction time becomes slower. Some impairment of concentration and memory may also occur.

**Vision:** visual acuity decreases. Dryness of the eye tissues may be problematic.

**Sleep:** more awakening during the night may affect the overall quality of sleep.

**Heart and blood vessels:** decrease in the distendibility of arteries ("hardening of arteries") leads to the tendency to raised blood pressure. Increase in fatty deposits within arteries contributes to circulatory insufficiency.

**Colon:** muscle function and tone decrease and elimination may be impaired.

**Urinary:** frequent urination and "stress incontinence" of urine may occur.

**Stomach:** decreased gastric (stomach) motility leads to delayed emptying and poor digestion. An increase in stomach acid may interfere with the absorption of iron and vitamin B12.

**BELOW** *Age need not be an obstacle to strenuous physical exercise, if you look after yourself.*

## STRATEGIES FOR GOOD HEALTH

One encouraging fact about aging is that when we are about 50 years old, we still have a chance to undo some of the damage we have done to ourselves during five decades of living. This is because the human body is more resilient and more capable of healing than we can ever imagine. In addition, we have the benefit of the marvelous advances in medical knowledge, technology, and practice. This combination should enable us to age healthfully, graciously, and joyfully.

**ABOVE** *Rediscover pastimes from your youth, such as cycling, swimming, or rambling.*

### EXERCISE

Slow-moving, stretching exercises, done with attention on the movements in synchronization with regular breathing, are less liable to cause injury than high-impact (or even some "low-impact") aerobic exercises. This is why many women over 50 choose yoga: it keeps them flexible, encourages body-mind awareness, promotes relaxation, and helps them with stress management.

The mini-workout on page 36 is a good example of this approach, and you will find the warm-ups on page 35 beneficial. In addition, try to also do some aerobic form of exercise, such as brisk walking, cycling, or dancing, three times a week.

**ABOVE** *Good habits formed in youth will stand you in good stead in later life.*

Straight spine

Keep stomach tucked in

Hands on the mat

Straight legs

**LEFT** *Yoga is gentle but effective, and keeps both body and mind in good condition.*

## NUTRITION

In addition to the information on pages 20–31, the following points are noteworthy as they seem to take on greater significance as we age:

❖ Water is vital for preventing spinal discs from drying out, for helping to keep the skin well moisturized, and for preventing constipation, bladder infection, and dehydration which is a major cause of preventable aging.

❖ Vitamin B12 is crucial for helping to maintain the ability to remember and concentrate, and to maintain balance.

❖ Vitamin E can help to preserve youthful looks by slowing down cellular aging, easing menopausal discomforts, and keeping blood pressure within normal limits, as well as maintaining healthy circulation.

**ABOVE** *Drinking plenty of water prevents the aging effects of dehydration.*

**RIGHT** *Foods that are high in nucleic acids will make you look and feel younger than your years.*

❖ Calcium helps to prevent osteoporosis and it is also useful in promoting good quality sleep.

❖ Iron is essential for the health of the circulatory and immune systems. It is often deficient in the diet of many older adults.

❖ Selenium helps preserve the youthful elasticity of tissues, alleviates hot flushes and other menopausal discomforts, and possibly helps in neutralizing certain carcinogens (cancer-causing agents). Selenium and vitamin E are synergistic, working together and reinforcing each other.

❖ Zinc helps to preserve mental alertness and contributes to the health of the circulatory and immune systems.

❖ Nucleic acids. Aging is thought by some experts to be partly attributable to the degeneration of the millions of cells of which the human body is composed. Although cells reproduce themselves, they alter with each successive reproduction, bringing about the deterioration that results in aging. This process can be influenced to some extent if the cells are provided with certain nourishing substances called "nucleic acids." You can actually look and feel considerably younger than your biological age if your diet is rich in this nutrient.

**LEFT** *Good nutrition is as important in later life as at any other time.*

Food sources abundant in nucleic acids include asparagus, bran, chicken liver, fish (especially anchovies, salmon, and sardines), mushrooms, oatmeal, onions, spinach, and wheat germ. It is best to avoid refined flour and sugar, tobacco, too much coffee and tea, carbonated drinks and sodas, and fried and processed foods.

**ABOVE** *Cut down on tea and coffee, and try to avoid sugar and unrefined flour.*

❖ Fat. By decreasing the fat content of your diet, you can help to protect yourself from high blood cholesterol, make it easier to control your weight. You may also decrease your risk of breast cancer.

## TIME FOR LIFE

You have finally "retired" and you want to celebrate your new-found freedom. You plan to do all the things you have been wanting or needing to do, but for which you have never had the time. The sad reality for many women who retire, however, is that after the initial euphoria of having unlimited time and leisure, a sense of purposelessness begins to emerge. The transition from this to depression can be extremely swift though not painless.

You need not be one of these depressed women. There are few things sadder and more destructive than boredom and loneliness. While there is still time, preferably when you are still young and energetic,

begin to prepare yourself for later life by developing a hobby or other pursuit that you can continue when you are no longer part of the work force outside the home. You can develop an interest that will benefit you financially later in life. This can be anything from studying the craft of writing and writing articles for publication to making hand-painted greeting cards to sell. Don't allow the calendar to control your life; if you have a lifelong dream of graduating, fulfil it by going to college and studying for a degree.

Many women do volunteer work at various organizations. Their contribution is invaluable and greatly appreciated. Giving of their time and of themselves helps them

to feel needed and this is good for their overall self-esteem. Venturing outside of the home and being with other people counteracts loneliness and helps to prevent anxiety and depression. It also provides some exercise and perhaps an opportunity to share mealtimes with others. This is useful since many older adults lack the motivation to prepare proper, nutritious meals when they are eating alone. Consider packing a picnic lunch occasionally and inviting a friend to share it with you in a nearby park or garden. The fresh air will do wonders for your appetite and spirits, and so will the companionship.

Most communities have centers for people who are 50 and older.

**ABOVE** *Gardening is a pastime that is physically and mentally stimulating, and can be a very sociable hobby, too.*

They offer a variety of classes including ballroom dancing, exercises of various kinds, painting, pottery, and creative writing. It is well worth looking into these possibilities, not only because of the opportunities for keeping constructively occupied, but also because of the socialization these classes offer. You might also consider instructing one such class, if you have the necessary expertise to do so.

We often tend to be preoccupied with what time is doing to us and give little thought about what we are doing with time. We are also

LEFT *Seek out companionship and don't be afraid to ask for a visit from family and friends.*

BELOW *After retirement you have the time to rediscover the real you and to please yourself without having to justify yourself to anyone.*

inclined to depend too much on others to give us confirmation of our worth.

Those who are the healthiest and happiest are the ones who have kept themselves physically active and mentally stimulated throughout their later lives. They have not permitted the calendar to dictate to them how old they are and they have not allowed others to determine their true worth. They are aging with health and dignity and independence. You can, too.

# 12 WHAT CAN GO WRONG

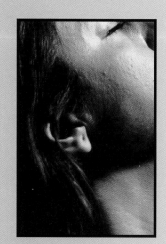

EVEN THE BEST CARED FOR MACHINE CAN AND DOES BREAK DOWN AND ITS PARTS WEAR OUT. THE HUMAN BODY, WHICH IS THE MOST INTRICATELY DESIGNED MACHINE IN EXISTENCE, IS NO EXCEP-TION. IN FACT, TAKING INTO ACCOUNT THE MANY ASSAULTS AGAINST WHICH IT HAS TO DEFEND ITSELF, IT IS AMAZING THAT IT RECOVERS AS OFTEN AS IT DOES. BELOW ARE 13 ILLNESSES TO WHICH WOMEN APPEAR PARTICULARLY VULNERABLE. THESE ARE CYSTITIS, CANCER (OF THE BREAST, CERVIX, OVARIES, UTERUS, LUNGS, AND COLON), HEART DISEASE AND STROKE, LUPUS, ME, MS, AND OSTEO-POROSIS. HOWEVER, PREVENTATIVE MEASURES CAN BE TAKEN TO REDUCE THE RISK OF DEVELOPING ANY OF THESE ILLNESSES DURING OUR LIVES.

## CYSTITIS

Cystitis is inflammation of the bladder. It is usually secondary to an ascending urinary tract infection. Its chief symptoms are frequent and painful urination.

### RISK FACTORS

Women are more vulnerable to cystitis than men because of their shorter urethra (canal extending from the bladder to the outside). The urethra in men measures 8–9 in (20–23 cm), whereas in women it is a mere $1\frac{1}{2}$ in (4 cm). This reduced distance between bladder and external environment facilitates contamination from the vagina and the anus. Sexually active and pregnant women are the most susceptible to this infection.

Other factors increasing the risk of cystitis are:
❖ Poorly fitting diaphragms used for contraception, because their pressure on the bladder may prevent complete emptying.
❖ Spermicides, because they seem to increase the vaginal acidity or alkalinity and alter normal vagina flora.

ABOVE *Be aware of the possible side-effects of your chosen method of contraception.*

## PREVENTATIVE MEASURES

To help to prevent cystitis and other urinary tract infections, the following measures are suggested:

❖ Wipe yourself from front to back, not vice versa, after urinating or having a bowel movement.

❖ Shower rather than take a bath, to prevent irritation and contamination of the urethra.

❖ Avoid taking bubble baths, which can cause irritation of the urethra.

❖ Wear cotton underpants, which are more absorbent than those made with synthetic material.

❖ Avoid wearing pantyhose with pants because they trap more moisture in the perineal area.

❖ Wash yourself well before having sexual intercourse.

*LEFT Try not to use any perfumed products and avoid putting bubbles in your bath — it is often best to have a shower instead.*

❖ Drink at least 4–6 pints (2-3 liters) of fluid a day to ensure good urinary output.

❖ Avoid wearing particularly tight jeans and pants.

❖ Avoid lounging about in a wet bathing suit.

❖ If you have a history of cystitis, avoid using feminine hygiene sprays, perfumed toilet paper, soap, and sanitary towels.

❖ Acidifying the urine does decrease the rate of bacterial multiplication. Traditionally, cranberry juice and ascorbic acid have been used for this purpose. Current studies however, indicate that neither of these adequately reduces urinary pH. Commercial cranberry juice, for example, does not usually contain a high enough concentration to reduce pH, unless you drink copious amounts of it. Include prunes, plums, cranberries, and whole grains in your diet.

❖ Avoid carbonated beverages, anything containing bicarbonate of soda or baking powder, and also olives and pickles, as these have an alkalining effect.

*BELOW Even if you are enjoying yourself on the beach with friends, try not to hang around with a wet bathing suit on.*

## BREAST CANCER

Cancer of the breast is one of the most common major cancers, second only to lung cancer. The psychological impact of breast cancer is far-reaching, embracing not only the prospect of death but also altered body image and self-esteem, and disruption in family relationships.

### CAUSES

The cause of breast cancer is still essentially unknown, but risk factors include:

❖ Family health history.

❖ Excessive exposure of breast tissue to radiation.

❖ Early menarch (first menstrual period) and late menopause.

❖ High dietary fat intake.

❖ Prolonged use of oral contraceptives.

### FOR BEST PROGNOSIS

Two tactics that may help to reduce breast cancer risk in some women are regular exercise and avoiding excessive alcohol consumption. For the majority of women, however, the best means of preventing breast cancer is through early detection: either by a mammography or by a monthly breast self-examination.

RIGHT *Studies suggest that prolonged use of oral contraceptives might increase the risk of breast cancer in some women.*

## BREAST SELF-EXAMINATION

Self-examination of your breasts should be done once a month, shortly after the menstrual period has ended. After menopause, continue to check your breasts monthly. If you find any abnormality, such as a thickening or lump, see your doctor immediately.

**I** Stand in front of a mirror. Inspect both breasts for anything unusual, such as puckering, dimpling, retraction of the nipples, scaling of the skin, discharge from the nipples, or lack of symmetry.

**2** Clasp your hands behind your head and press your hands forward. You should feel your chest muscles tighten. Observe the shape and contour of your breasts.

**3** Next, press your hands firmly on your hips, bow slightly toward the mirror and pull your shoulders and elbows forward. Again, look at the shape and contour of the breasts.

You may want to do the next two steps in the shower as your fingers can glide easily over the soapy skin, making it easy to concentrate on the texture of the skin.

**4** Raise your left arm. Use three or four fingers of your right hand to explore your left breast firmly, carefully, and thoroughly. Beginning at the outer edge, press the flat part of your fingers in small circles, moving systematically around the breast. Feel for nodules or other irregularities. Pay special attention to the area between the breast and the armpit (axilla), making sure you check the armpit itself as well.

**5** Gently squeeze the nipple and look for a discharge. Repeat steps 4 and 5 with the other breast.

If you wish to do steps 4 and 5 while lying down; lie flat on your back, with a pillow or folded towel under your left shoulder (this position flattens the breast and facilitates examination). Use the same circular motions that were described above. Then repeat the process with the other breast.

## CERVICAL CANCER

This refers to cancer of the cervix or neck of the uterus (womb). Risk factors include:

❖ Having sex at an early age, frequent sexual intercourse with multiple partners, being with a partner who has genital warts or other sexually transmitted diseases (STDs).

❖ An early first pregnancy, having many children, or untreated chronic cervicitis (inflammation of the cervix).

❖ Women whose partners have a history of penile or prostrate cancer. (Jewish women and celibate women have a very low risk.)

❖ 25–40-year-old women are at high risk of "carcinoma in situ," in which malignant cell changes affect the superficial layer of tissues.

❖ 40–60-year-old women are at greater risk of invasive cancer.

**BELOW** *Know your body. It is always worth taking advice on anything that is not "normal" for you.*

### PREVENTION

Primary prevention is related to good health practices such as avoiding vaginal and cervical infections, or obtaining early treatment if they develop. Responsible sexual relations and the use of condoms to control transmission of STDs help to prevent cervical cancer.

Regular cervical smears are an excellent means of detecting pre-cancerous or cancerous conditions. This test is particularly important because cervical carcinoma in situ is almost 100 percent curable.

## OVARIAN CANCER

This is the most lethal gynecological malignancy. Women that are most at risk are:

❖ Over 40 years of age.

❖ Those with a family history of the disease.

❖ Women who have never borne a child.

❖ Those with a history of heavy menstruation or dysmenorrhea.

There are other possible risk factors that are still under research:

❖ Obesity, due to a diet high in animal fat.

❖ The use of talcum powder, which may contain an ingredient chemically related to asbestos. (Some women regularly dust their perineum with talcum powder and use it on sanitary towels.)

### PREVENTION

In addition to refraining from the use of talcum powder, and reducing the intake of animal fat in the diet, early detection is an important way to help prevent ovarian cancer. This is particularly important for women in the high risk zones so doctors and other health professionals often recommend routine pelvic examinations. It may be useful to have a transvaginal ultrasound and, if the results are suspicious, a Doppler study also. This is a non-invasive technique that uses special ultrasound equipment. It is also known as Doppler ultrasonography.

## UTERINE CANCER

This cancer can occur either in the cervix (*see cervical cancer page 113*) or in the endometrium (lining of the uterus). Endometrial cancer is the most common pelvic cancer in women.

❖ It generally appears in women between the ages of 50 and 70 years and is more common in women who have had few, or no, children.

❖ It occurs more frequently in women who have had an excess of estrogen in their body, particularly if their progesterone levels are also low. As well as hormone therapy, obesity may raise estrogen levels.

### SYMPTOMS

The most common symptom of endometrial cancer is irregular bleeding, with or without abdominal discomfort. Women past menopause who experience this symptom should report it to their doctor immediately for further investigation. Women still menstruating should regard highly irregular periods and/or bleeding between periods as suspicious and consult a doctor.

### PREVENTION/ TREATMENT

When detected in its early stages – when it is still confined to the uterus and has not spread outside the pelvis – endometrial cancer is almost 100 percent curable if treated promptly. Treatment usually entails a hysterectomy (surgical removal of the uterus) and removal of both Fallopian tubes and ovaries.

## LUNG CANCER

This cancer is uncommon in women under the age of 40, but the incidence of lung cancer is rising at a faster rate than that of any other type of cancer. There are several types of lung cancer, the most common being squamous cell carcinoma, small cell carcinoma, adenocarcinoma, and large cell carcinoma. There are many factors that contribute to the occurrence of this disease including coming into contact with carcinogens, which include inhaled toxins such as asbestos and various pollutants, and genetic predisposition to the development of cancer.

The most common cause of lung cancer, however, is smoking: seven out of eight cases of lung cancer are caused by years or decades of cigarette smoking. The more cigarettes smoked per day, and the younger the starting age, the higher the risk. Smoking also lowers the levels of beta carotene and vitamins A and C, which are among the antioxidants that give protection against many cancers.

### WARNING SIGNALS

Signs to alert you to the possibility of the development or presence of lung cancer include:

⊙ Any changes in your breathing pattern.

⊙ Persistent cough.

⊙ Sputum streaked with blood, or rust-colored or purulent sputum.

⊙ Coughing up blood.

⊙ Pain in the chest, shoulder, or arm.

⊙ Difficulty in breathing out, or in proportion to effort expended.

⊙ Recurring episodes of bronchitis or pneumonia. You should consult your doctor immediately if any of these warning signs appear.

**RIGHT** *The sooner you seek help, the sooner you can have your fears allayed – or begin an appropriate course of treatment.*

❖ Measures to reduce the inhalation of cigarette smoke by children and other young people, such as school-based programs to promote tobacco-free environments and prevent tobacco use (including information on the risks of oral cancer).

❖ Emphasizing the cessation of smoking during pregnancy in antenatal classes.

## COLON CANCER

Colon cancer is the third most common cancer, after lung and breast cancers. The risk factors include:

❖ Family history of colon cancer.

❖ Being over 40 years of age.

❖ Ulcerative colitis (inflammation of the colon).

❖ High-fat, low-residue diet (high in refined foods).

❖ Living in highly industrialized, urban societies.

### PREVENTION

Early detection is the best preventative measure. It is advisable for women over 40 years of age to be given a yearly digital rectal examination (the doctor examines the rectum with gloved fingers) and, for women over 50 years of age, an examination by protoscope (an instrument to inspect the rectum). Reducing the amount of fat and refined foods, and increasing fiber intake in the diet will help to reduce the risks of colon cancer.

## CIGARETTE SMOKING

Heavy smokers – those who smoke more than 25 cigarettes a day – have 20 times the risk of developing lung cancer as non-smokers do. Although stopping smoking lowers this risk, it takes 15–20 years for a smoker's lungs to clear enough to become like a non-smoker's.

Recent studies also suggest that passive smoking (second-hand smoke inhaled from the area surrounding an active smoker) may account for up to five percent of lung cancer. Living or working in a highly polluted, or even radioactive, area may cause some lung cancers.

## PREVENTION

The habit of smoking is rapidly increasing among schoolchildren, particularly among girls. Despite a new public awareness of the outcome of habitual smoking and the negative image of smoking, women and girls do not seem to be heeding the message because smoking is so addictive. The key in prevention, therefore, is to stop people from starting to smoke.

Lung cancer is preventable. Long-term objectives to reduce the prevalence of smoking among women should include:

❖ Tobacco control interventions that specifically target women.

## HEART DISEASE

The number one killer of women is not cancer. It is heart and blood vessel (cardiovascular) disease. It accounts for more deaths than breast, lung, and cervical cancer combined. One in nine women between the ages of 45 and 64 and one in three women 65 and over has one of the types of heart or blood vessel disease.

### RISK FACTORS

The factors putting women at risk of heart disease are:

❖ Family history of heart disease.
❖ Smoking (smoking while taking oral contraceptives increases the risk by almost 40 times).

❖ High cholesterol.
❖ High blood pressure.
❖ Diabetes.
❖ Lack of exercise.
❖ Being overweight.
❖ High homocysteine levels.
(*see vitamin B6, page 23*).

### PREVENTION

In perhaps no other disease are changes in lifestyle more important. The changes to make are to:

❖ Stop smoking.
❖ Exercise regularly.
❖ Choose a "healthy heart" diet that is low in fat and salt and high in fiber and essential nutrients.
❖ Attain and maintain a healthy body weight.

❖ Learn and regularly practice effective stress management strategies *(see page 70)*.
❖ Ask your doctor to check your blood pressure and cholesterol level regularly.

**ABOVE** *Use your heart and keep it fit. Take plenty of exercise.*

### BLOOD THINNING

If you modify your lifestyle habits, as suggested above, the benefits will outweigh those of regularly taking blood-thinning agents such as aspirin. One of the risks of continually thinning the blood is increasing the possibility of bleeding (hemorrhage).

However, blood-thinning is benefical as it helps to prevent the formation of blood clots. There are safer, more natural, methods of blood-thinning including adding omega-3 fatty acids from oily fish to your diet, and also raw garlic and onions that have protective properties (chewing parsley will freshen your breath afterward). Discuss these alternatives with your doctor if you are taking blood-thinning agents.

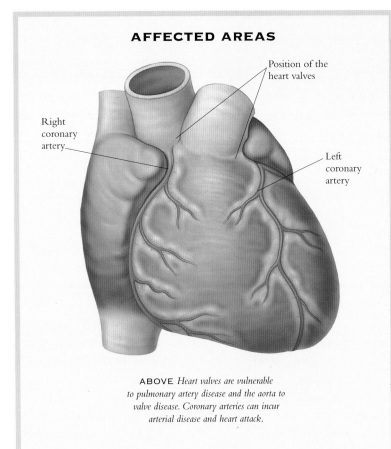

### AFFECTED AREAS

Position of the heart valves

Right coronary artery

Left coronary artery

**ABOVE** *Heart valves are vulnerable to pulmonary artery disease and the aorta to valve disease. Coronary arteries can incur arterial disease and heart attack.*

## HRT AND HEART DISEASE

Women rarely report symptoms of heart disease before menopause. When estrogen levels decrease in the years around menopause, the risk of heart disease increases. Hormone replacement therapy (HRT) provides a measure of protection from heart disease. HRT, however, is not for everyone, and it is suspected of putting some women at risk of developing certain cancers. If you are considering HRT, do discuss the pros and cons with your doctor.

*LEFT HRT might help prevent heart disease. However, make sure you understand all the implications if you plan to take it.*

## STROKE

Strokes affect hundreds of thousands of people every year and the effects can be devastating. A stroke occurs when a blood vessel delivering oxygen and nutrients to part of the brain becomes clogged or bursts. Nerve cells in that area cease to work properly and the body functions they control also stop working normally. This can result in difficulty in speaking, inability to walk and perhaps to use an arm.

## RISK FACTORS

Some risk factors can be treated but others cannot. Treatable factors are:

❖ High blood pressure.
❖ Heart disease.
❖ Cigarette smoking.
❖ High red blood cell count.
❖ Transient ischaemic attacks. (TIAs) are strong predictors of a stroke, and are usually treated with drugs that ensure that blood clots do not form.

Risk factors that cannot be changed include:
❖ Age, because older people are at greater risk than the young.
❖ Previous strokes, as they increase the chances of having another one.
❖ Heredity.

Other factors, which are modifiable, indirectly increase the risk of stroke. They include:
❖ Elevated blood fats and cholesterol.
❖ Excessive alcohol intake.
❖ Physical inactivity.

*ABOVE The effects of stroke are upsetting, but, with a bit of practice, this woman has learned to walk again with the aid of a walking stick.*

❖ Obesity.
See also risk factors for cardiovascular disease on page 116.

## PREVENTION

Regular check-ups, which provide early detection, are, as with many of these diseases, your best protection. By taking a careful medical history, making an examination, and ordering certain tests, a doctor can usually predict features that predispose you to suffering a stroke. The preventative measures you can take are the same as for heart disease.

## LUPUS (SLE)

Systemic lupus erythematosus (SLE), which is commonly known as lupus, belongs to a class of diseases termed "autoimmune." This means that the body's immune system, which is designed to protect you from attack by foreign agents, turns instead against you. Lupus can affect many tissues and organs including the heart and blood vessels, kidneys, nervous system, lungs, joints, skin, and collagen – the "glue" that holds the body's cells together.

With the exception of disorders affecting the female reproductive system, no other illness targets females as much as lupus does. The ratio of females to males with SLE is six to one, and during the child-bearing years nine to 10 women for each man develop SLE. In fact, SLE has a predilection for adult women between the teen years and the 40s.

RIGHT *One of the symptoms of the chameleon-like disease lupus is mood swings.*

## SIGNS AND SYMPTOMS

SLE has been likened to a chameleon – always changing. Its manifestations mimic those of so many other illnesses that it is sometimes difficult to diagnose. Early SLE symptoms include:

❖ Persistent aching and stiffness of joints, mainly those of the fingers, wrists, elbows, and knees.

❖ An acute infection.

❖ General malaise.

❖ Fatigue and weakness.

❖ Mild fever – about 100°F (37.7°C).

❖ A rash.

❖ Mood swings.

There are now special tests to help in the diagnosis of SLE. Lupus erythematosus is a blood test used to diagnose and monitor treatment. Antinuclear Antibody test determines the presence of antinuclear antibodies (ANA), an unusual type of antibody found in the blood of almost all people that have lupus.

RIGHT *Women of all ages, particularly those in the child-bearing years, are more susceptible to lupus than men are.*

## FLARES AND REMISSIONS

Flares, or exacerbations, are periods when the illness increases in severity or when the symptoms recur. Factors contributing to SLE flares are:

❖ Exposure to heat and sun.

❖ Stress.

❖ Infections.

❖ Some medications (such as certain pain-relievers, oral contraceptives, anti-seizure, and anti-depressant agents).

Many lupus sufferers experience periods of remission in which their symptoms abate entirely or at least lessen in severity.

## LIVING WITH LUPUS

Many individuals diagnosed with lupus cope with the disease very well indeed, considering its unpredictability. Generally, the most successful of the treatment programs require:

❖ Taking prescribed medications faithfully, and not altering dosages without the doctor's consent.

❖ Exercising regularly, in accordance with your level of energy and "wellness."

❖ Obtaining adequate rest and relaxation.

❖ Adhering to a wholesome diet at all times.

❖ Practicing good dental hygiene and seeing your dentist regularly, at least twice a year.

❖ Avoiding unnecessary exposure to sunlight, halogen lamps, and fluorescent lights.

❖ Establishing and maintaining supportive relationships.

❖ Limiting contact with people who have infections; and washing hands frequently.

**RIGHT** *As with so many health issues, gentle exercise is part of an overall treatment program for lupus.*

## ME (MYALGIC ENCEPHALOMYELITIS)

**M**yalgic refers to muscle pain; encephalo pertains to the brain; myelo denotes inflammation of the spinal cord. ME is thus an illness that affects the brain, muscles, and nervous system, causing inflammation and pain. Once known as "yuppie flu" in the UK, it is known in the USA as Chronic Fatigue Syndrome (CFS) or Chronic Fatigue and Immune Deficiency Syndrome (CFIDS). It can be a seriously debilitating condition and may last for months or even years.

**BELOW** *Once dismissed as being "all in the mind," ME is now taken seriously and treated as a real, physical illness.*

### CAUSES

Controversy persists regarding the causes of ME, but research in Britain and Canada has focused on the role of enteroviruses as the primary contributing factor. These are viruses that infect the intestines and sometimes spread to other parts of the body, especially the central nervous system.

### SYMPTOMS

Many of the symptoms of ME disappear over time, although some persist for a number of years. The most striking symptom is severe, incapacitating fatigue. For a diagnosis of ME to be made, the fatigue must have persisted for six months and must have been accompanied by other symptoms:

❖ Aching muscles and joints.
❖ Sore throat.
❖ Painful lymph glands.
❖ Fever and headache.
❖ Muscle weakness.
❖ Sleep disturbances.
❖ Mental fatigue.
❖ Difficulty in concentrating.
❖ Mood swings.

**LEFT** *Chronic fatigue is the main symptom of ME but it is always accompanied by others, including aching joints, fever, and mood swings.*

**ABOVE** *Even when you can't be bothered to cook, try to maintain nutritional balance and include fresh fruit and vegetables in your diet.*

## TREATMENTS

As yet, no foolproof treatment for ME exists. Some anecdotal successes have been reported with the use of a wide range of therapies, including antiviral drugs and those designed to regulate the immune system, and also various holistic remedies.

However, some of these treatments may be of no value to you, because their efficacy is based only on reports patients have made to their doctors. Such treatments have not been subjected to clinical trials. Others are potentially harmful: for example, ME sufferers tend to react badly to many nutritional supplements that people with other illnesses can take without problems. Also, with prolonged use, some drugs may have adverse effects while others may create dependency. It is therefore best to check with your doctor before trying any treatment or combination of treatments for ME.

**BELOW** *Learn to listen to your body and keep exercise within comfortable limits.*

Health authorities, however, normally recommend the following as a prudent approach to living with ME:

❖ Consult a reputable doctor to rule out other conditions that may present symptoms that are similar to ME. Have periodic checks for other diseases, some of which may be difficult to detect but could be treatable.

❖ Do not over-exert yourself, since this tends to aggravate symptoms. Obtain plenty of rest and relaxation to conserve your energy *(see breathwork page 40, mindwork page 50, and stress management page 70).*

❖ Exercise only as much as you can comfortably tolerate. Develop a sort of "fine tuning-in" to your body's cues.

❖ Eat adequately *(see page 20).*

# MS
## (MULTIPLE SCLEROSIS)

Multiple (disseminated) Sclerosis, or MS, is the most common nervous system disease affecting young adults, occurring slightly more frequently in women than in men. It is classified (like lupus) as an autoimmune disease.

In MS, the "myelin sheath" is affected. This is the term given to the coating around nerve fibers, similar to insulation around an electrical cord. When the sheath is damaged, as it is in MS, messages from the brain to the muscles may be slowed down or not get through at all.

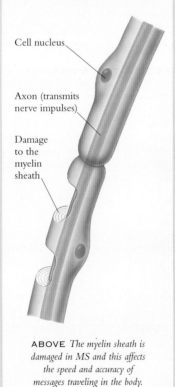

## DAMAGED NERVE FIBERS

Cell nucleus

Axon (transmits nerve impulses)

Damage to the myelin sheath

**ABOVE** *The myelin sheath is damaged in MS and this affects the speed and accuracy of messages traveling in the body.*

## CAUSES

No one is sure what causes MS, and the disorder can be very problematic because its symptoms are variable not only between one sufferer and another, but also in the same person at different times. Many neurologists (specialists in nervous system diseases) are convinced that a virus is to blame. Other doctors believe that MS is a disease of blood vessels and that the neurological damage is due to blood leaking into the brain. Still others have found evidence to link MS to faulty fat metabolism.

There does seem to be a genetic factor; those who have relatives with the disease are eight times more likely to contract MS.

## EXACERBATIONS

Factors that aggravate MS symptoms and contribute to exacerbations include:

❖ Emotional upsets.
❖ Infections.
❖ Over-exertion and fatigue.
❖ Injuries.
❖ Surgery.
❖ Pregnancy.

## LIVING WITH MS

There is no specific therapy for MS but careful attention to the following will contribute to living a happy, productive life:

❖ Exercise regularly, according to your level of functioning and overall energy.

❖ Avoid becoming too fatigued. Make sure that you obtain adequate rest and relaxation (*see chapters 4, 5, and 7*).

❖ Learn and practice effective stress management techniques (*see chapter 7*).

❖ Ensure that your diet is adequate (*see pages 20–31*). Nutrients particularly important for MS sufferers include:

Vitamin B5 (pantothenic acid), found in avocado, brewer's yeast, broccoli, brown rice, cabbage, cauliflower, filbert nuts, green vegetables, pulses, milk, mushrooms, pecan nuts, potatoes, unrefined vegetable oils, wheat germ, and whole grains.

Stress greatly increases the need for this and other B vitamins. In fact, in experimental animals, a lack of this nutrient actually resulted in a loss of myelin sheath. When the nutrient is furnished,

ABOVE *While there is as yet no cure for MS, a diet rich in vitamin B5, essential fatty acids, and lecithin may help relieve the symptoms.*

content of the brain and myelin sheath of MS victims. These tissues are normally high in lecithin.

MS is most common in countries where the diet is high in saturated fat, and the blood lecithin level consequently decreased.

Good dietary sources of lecithin include eggs (particularly free-range eggs), cold-pressed vegetable oils (such as safflower, soy, and sunflower), soybeans, nuts, whole-wheat cereals, wheat germ, and meats such as liver and heart.

❖ In some communities additional resources exist in the form of MS support groups and organizations. These will be able to give you in-depth information on this illness. Check to see if there is one in your community.

however, a marked improvement in humans has been reported.

**Essential fatty acids:** obtainable from evening primrose oil, (*see chapter 9, PMS*). EFAs have been used to treat MS (*see bibliography page 126*).

**Lecithin:** is a substance that improves fat metabolism. It breaks down fat and cholesterol in the blood so that they may be utilized effectively by the body's cells. Autopsy studies have revealed a marked decrease in the lecithin

BELOW *MS is an unpredictable and therefore frightening illness. Talking to fellow sufferers can go a long way toward helping you cope.*

## OSTEOPOROSIS

Osteoporosis is a bone-loss disorder that affects mainly postmenopausal women, at the rate of about one in four. The predominant feature is decreased bone density, brought about because bone is breaking down faster than it is being formed. The greatest losses occur in spongy bone, rather than in compact bone. Particularly serious are those losses in the spine and thigh bones. The spinal bones (vertebrae) become compressed by the weight of the body and fractures can occur. These can reduce a person's height by several inches.

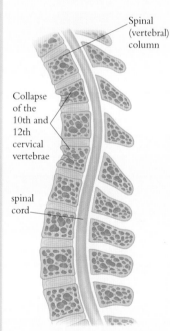

### DAMAGE TO BONES

Spinal (vertebral) column

Collapse of the 10th and 12th cervical vertebrae

spinal cord

*ABOVE With osteoporosis, loss of height results from the collapse of the vertebrae, which become compressed.*

RIGHT *Weight-bearing exercise may prevent the onset of osteoporosis – and that includes dancing.*

### CAUSES

The exact cause of loss of bone mass is unknown, but older women are particularly vulnerable as after the menopause their ovaries are no longer producing estrogen. This hormone is particularly useful in helping to maintain bone mass. Other factors associated with osteoporosis in postmenopausal women include:

❖ Heredity.
❖ The amount of bone mass at skeletal maturity.
❖ Lack of calcium.
❖ Hormones (diminished estrogen production is the most important hormonal factor).
❖ Removal of the ovaries.

Other risk factors that are not controllable include:

❖ Thin or small bones.
❖ Having Caucasian or Asiatic ethnicity.
❖ Confinement to bed.
❖ Not having borne children.

Risk factors that are actually controllable include:

❖ Excessive caffeine intake.
❖ Excessive alcohol intake.
❖ High protein intake.
❖ High salt (sodium) intake.
❖ High phosphate intake (from the use of carbonated beverages, for example).
❖ Little or no weight-bearing exercise at all.
❖ A sedentary lifestyle.
❖ Smoking.
❖ Excessive exercise.

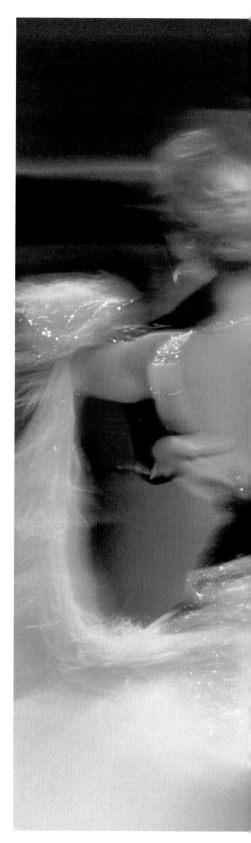

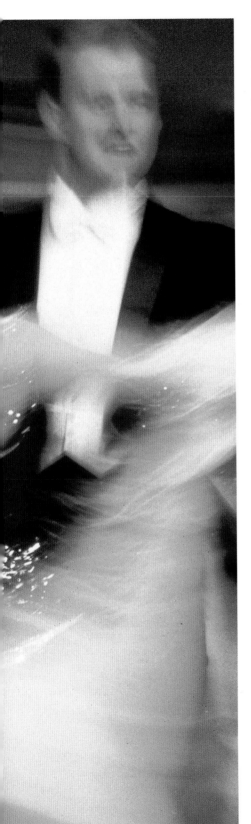

## PREVENTION AND TREATMENT

Exercise appears to help in the development of original bone mass and also in retarding bone loss in later life. It may even actually increase bone mass in older women. Weight-bearing exercise, such as walking and dancing, is especially important.

The role of nutrition in osteoporosis is related chiefly to dietary calcium intake. This tends to be lower in older women, compared with younger females, and is often aggravated by decreased intestinal absorption. The level of vitamin D in the body may also play an important role in calcium absorption.

Other nutrients pertinent to the prevention of osteoporosis include:
**Boron**: this is a trace mineral that has been shown to safeguard calcium in the body. It appears to be necessary for activating vitamin D, as well as certain hormones, including estrogen. Good sources of boron include fresh fruits, particularly grapes; fresh vegetables; and dried fruit.

**Fluorine (fluoride)**: this mineral, which is vital to a person's general well-being, works with calcium to strengthen the body's bones. Organic fluorine is found in almonds, beet tops, carrots, garlic, green vegetables, milk, cheese, oat flakes, and sunflower seeds. It is also naturally present in hard water.

**Magnesium, silicon, and zinc:** these nutrients are all of value in retarding or preventing osteoporosis as they help form and preserve healthy bones *(see page 27–28)*.

The administration of estrogen to treat osteoporosis may require precautions in postmenopausal women who may be susceptible to cancer. See the section on hormone replacement therapy and heart disease on page 117.

### HELPFUL HINT

Stop smoking. Smoking has been shown to be the cause of accelerated bone loss. It also lowers estrogen levels in the body.

**ABOVE** *Boosting your intake of boron and fluorine will help sustain bone mass as these minerals both work alongside calcium.*

# BIBLIOGRAPHY

ABURDENE, PATRICIA, and JOHN NAISBITT. *Megatrends for Women* New York: Villard Books, 1992.

ALLEN, KAREN MOSES, PH.D, R.N., and JANICE MITCHELL PHILLIPS, PH.D, R.N. *Women's Health Across the Lifespan A Comprehensive Perspective.* Philadelphia: Lippincott, 1997.

AMERICAN HEART ASSOCIATION AND AMERICAN CANCER SOCIETY. *Living Well, Staying Well.* New York: Times Books, 1996.

AMERICAN MEDICAL ASSOCIATION. *Complete Guide to Woman's Health.* New York: Random House, 1996.

AMERICAN PSYCHIATRIC ASSOCIATION. *Diagnostic and Statistical Manual of Mental Disorders: 4th ed.* (DSM IV).

AMMER, CHRISTINE. *The New A to Z of Women's Health.* New York and Oxford: Facts on File, 1989.

ARGULE, MICHAEL. *The Psychology of Interpersonal Behavior: 3rd ed.* New York: Penguin Books, 1978.

BANVILLE, THOMAS G. *How to Listen – How to Be Heard.* Chicago: Nelson Hall, 1978.

BLACK, JOYCE M,. M.S.N., R.N.C., and ESTHER MATASSARIN-JACOBS, PH.D., R.N., O.C.N. *Luckman and Sorensen's Medical-Surgical Nursing: 4th ed.* Philadelphia: W. B. Saunders, 1993.

BLAU, SHELDON PAUL, M.D., and DODI SCHULTZ. *Lupus: The Body Against Itself: ref. ed.* Garden City, New York: Doubleday, 1984.

BRAIKER, HARRIET, B., PH.D. *The Type E Woman.* Scarborough, Canada: The New American Library of Canada, 1987.

BRANDEN, NATHANIEL. *The Power of Self-Esteem.* Deerfield Beach, Florida: Health Communications, 1992.

- - - - -. *How to Raise your Self Esteem.* New York: Bantam Books, 1987.

BRENA, STEVEN F., M. D. *Yoga and Medicine.* Baltimore, Maryland: Penguin Books, 1972.

CARLSON, KAREN, J., M.D., STEPHANIE A EISENSTAT, M.D., and TERRA ZIPORYN, PH.D. *The Harvard Guide to Women's Health.* Cambridge, Massachusetts, and London, England: Harvard University Press, 1996.

CASTLEMAN, MICHAEL. *Nature's Cures.* Emmaus, Pennsylvania: Rodale Press, 1996.

COOLEY, MARILYN. *Checklist for a Working Wife.* New York: Doubleday, 1979.

DUMAS, LINDA, PH.D, R.N. guest ed. *The Nursing Clinics of North America,* Vol. 27, Number 4, Philadelphia: W.B. Saunders, 1992.

FANNING, TONY AND ROBBIE. *Get it All Done and Still be Human.* Radnor, Pennsylvania: Chilton Book Company, 1979.

FAST, JULIUS AND BARBARA. *Talking Between the Lines.* New York: Viking Press, 1979.

FELDER, DEBORAH G. *The 100 Most Influential Women of All Time.* New York: Carol Publishing Group, 1996.

FOLEY, DENISE, EILEEN NECHAS, and EDITORS OF "PREVENTION." *Women's Encyclopedia of Health & Emotional Healing.* Emmaus, Pennsylvania: Rodale Press, 1993.

FROMM, ERICH. *The Art of Loving.* New York: Bantam, 1956.

GRAHAM, JUDY. *Evening Primrose Oil.* Wellingborough, England: Thorsons, 1984.

GRAY, JOHN, PH.D. *Men Are From Mars, Women Are From Venus.* New York: HarperCollins, 1992.

HEALY, BERNADINE, M.D. *A New Prescription for Women's Health.* New York: Viking, 1995.

HECKHEIMER, ESTELLE, R.N., M.A. *Health Promotion of the Elderly in the Community.* Philadelphia: W.B. Saunders, 1989.

HICKLING, MEG, R.N. *Speaking of Sex.* Canada: Northstone, 1996.

HOFFMAN, EILEEN, M.D. *Our Health, Our Lives.* New York: Pocket Books, 1995.

KAPLAN, HAROLD E., M.D., and BENJAMIN J SADOCK, M.D. *Synopsis of Psychiatry: 6th ed.* Baltimore, Maryland: Williams & Wilkins, 1991.

LAZRUS, RICHARD S. *Patterns of Adjustment: 3rd ed.* New York: McGraw-Hill, 1976

LEBOEUF, MICHAEL. *Working Smart.* New York: McGraw-Hill, 1979.

LEWIS, JUDITH A., PH.D., R.N.C., F.R.A.N., and JUDITH BERNSTEIN, PH.D., R.N.C. *Woman's Health. A Relational Perspective Across the Life Cycle.* Boston and London: Jones and Bartlett, 1996.

LONSDORF, NANCY, M.D., VERONICA BUTLER, M.D., and MELANIE BROWN, PH.D. *A Woman's Best Medicine.* New York: Jeremy P. Tarcher/Putnam, 1993.

MACKENZIE, R. ALEC. *The Time Trap.* New York: McGraw-Hill, 1975.

MILLS, SIMON, M.A., and STEVEN J. FINANDO, PH.D. *Alternatives in Healing.* New York: New American Library, 1988.

MINDELL, EARL. *Earl Mindell's Vitamin Bible.* New York: Warner Books, 1979.

- - - . *Earl Mindell's Food as Medicine.* New York: Simon & Schuster, 1994.

- - -. *Earl Mindell's Anti-Aging Bible.* New York and London: Simon & Schuster, 1996.

MINISTRY OF HEALTH. *Baby's Best Chance.* Province of British Columbia, Canada: Ministry of Health, 1979.

MOFFATT, MARY JANE, and CHARLOTTE PAINTER, eds.

*Revelations. Dairies of Women.* New York: Random House, 1974.

MOGADAM, MICHAEL, M.D. *Choosing Foods for a Healthy Heart.* New York: Consumer Reports Books, 1993.

QUILLIAM, SUE, and IAN GROVE-STEPHENSEN. *How to Stay in Love.* London: Thorsons, 1988.

REICHMAN, JUDITH, M.D., *I'm Too Young to Get Old.* New York: Times Books, 1996.

ROSS, H.M. *Fighting Depression.* New York: Larchmont Books, 1975.

ROSSMAN, ISADORE, M.D. PH.D. *Looking Forward. The Complete Medical Guide to Successful Aging.* New York: E.P. Dutton, 1989.

SHAEVITZ, MARJORIE HANSEN. *The Superwoman Syndrome.* New York: Warner Books, 1984.

SHREEVE, CAROLINE, M.D. *The Premenstrual Syndrome.* Wellingborough, England: Thorsons, 1983.

SIMKIN, PENNY, P.T., JANET WHALLEY, R.N., B.S.N., and ANN KEPPLER, R.N., M.N. *Pregnancy, Childbirth and the Newborn. The Complete Guide.* Deephaven, Minnesota: Meadowbrook Press, 1991.

SIMONTON, O. CARL, M.D., STEPHANIE MATTHEWS-SIMONTON, and JAMES CREIGHTON. *Getting Well Again.* London: Bantam Books, 1980.

SNYDERMAN, NANCY L., M.D., and MARGARET BLACKSTONE. *Dr. Nancy Snyderman's Guide to Good Health.* New York: William Morrow and Company, 1996.

STANTON, ROSEMARY. *Eating for Peak Performance.* Sydney: Allen & Unwin, 1988.

SWEDO, SUSAN, M.D., and HENRIETTA LEONARD, M.D. *It's Not All In Your Head.* San Francisco: Harper SanFrancisco, 1996.

TASMAN, ALLAN, M.D., JERALD KAY, M.D., and JEFFREY A. LIEBERMAN, M.D. *Psychiatry: Vol. 2.* Philadelphia: W.B. Saunders, 1997.

TREBEN, MARIA. *Health from God's Garden.* Rochester, Vermont: Healing Arts Press, 1988.

VISCOTT, DAVID. *How to Live With Another Person.* New York: Arbor House, 1974.

WEIL, ANDREW, M.D. *Natural Health, Natural Medicine.* Boston: Houghton Mifflin, 1990.

- - -. *Spontaneous Healing.* New York: Alfred A. Knopf, 1995.

WELLER, STELLA, *The Breath Book.* London: Thorsons, 1999.

- - -. *Yoga for Long Life.* London: Thorsons, 1997.

- - -. *Pain-Free Periods.* London: Thorsons, 1993.

- - -. *Easy Pregnancy with Yoga.* London: Thorsons, 1991

- - -. *Santé immunitaire Naturelle.* Genèvre: Editions Jouvence, 1991.

- - -. *Super Healthy Hair, Skin & Nails.* London: Thorsons. 1991.

WITKIN, GEORGIA, PH.D. *The Female Stress Syndrome.* New York: Newmarket Press, 1991.

# INDEX

## ACKNOWLEDGMENTS

*I thank everyone who has helped me with this work. I am particularly grateful to Walter, Karl, and David; to Linda Howard, Carol MacFarlane, and Marjory Jardine; to Claire Musters and Jane Lanaway of Bridgewater Books, and to Debbie Thorpe, Donna Wood, and Sandy Breakwell of Godsfield Press.*